MORE THAN BAUHAUS
THE ARCHITECTURE OF THE WHITE CITY TEL AVIV
edited by Regina Stephan

MORE THAN BAUHAUS

THE ARCHITECTURE OF THE WHITE CITY TEL AVIV

This book "**More than Bauhaus – The Architecture of the White City Tel Aviv**" concludes the German-Israeli-Austrian students workshop "Spring School Tel Aviv. 100 Years Bauhaus 1919-2019. International research and design project on site".

The first part of the Workshop took place in the Bauhaus Dessau in November 2018: Bauhaus Open Studios – Teaching Models – A Project of the Stiftung Bauhaus Dessau in Cooperation with Hochschule Mainz, University of Applied Sciences.

The second part of the workshop took place in and was strongly supported by the White City Center in Tel Aviv in March 2019.

The correspondent exhibition as well as the film of the same name by Frithjof Heinrich and Malte Röthig was first presented in Mainz. It will be shown in Braunschweig, Chemnitz, Dessau, Hannover, Innsbruck, Jerusalem and Tel Aviv.

The Workshop was substantially subsidised by the German Federal Ministry of the Interior, Building and Community.

Edited by Regina Stephan
Translation from the German and copy editing: Timothy Connell, Verbatim, London

Design & Image editing: Anke von Schalscha-Ehrenfeld
Front Cover, photo: meunierd/Shutterstock.com, 2016
Back Cover, photo: Oleg Zaslavsky/Shutterstock.com

ISBN 978-3-88778-560-4
Publication © by Spurbuchverlag 1. print run 2019
Am Eichenhügel 4, 96148 Baunach, Germany

AADR – Art, Architecture and Design Research publishes research with an emphasis on the relationship between critical theory and creative practice

AADR Curatorial Editor: Rochus Urban Hinkel, Stockholm & Nuremberg

Production: pth-mediaberatung GmbH, Würzburg

INDEX

FOREWORD
More than Bauhaus: The White City Tel Aviv

This year, 2019, marks one hundred years since the foundation of the Bauhaus. Germany has therefore taken the opportunity to celebrate this anniversary with partners across the world. The Federal Ministry of the Interior, Building and Community (BMI) has pledged its support for a wholesale appreciation of the Bauhaus in its centenary year in the form of various projects. Among them, the project "More than Bauhaus: the Architecture of Tel Aviv's White City" can be singled out as a very special one indeed.

When the Bauhaus was founded in Weimar in 1919, a number of young pioneers from the worlds of architecture, art and culture came together to collaborate on the development of new principles for design and living. With its progressive structure, interdisciplinary approach and love of experimentation, the Bauhaus attracted international masters, such as Walter Gropius, Ludwig Mies van der Rohe, Hannes Meyer, Paul Klee, Wassily Kandinsky, Johannes Itten, László Moholy-Nagy and Oskar Schlemmer. Like hardly any other twentieth-century movement, the Bauhaus has had a lasting influence on architecture, design, urban planning and the art and crafts sector.

The Nazis banned the school in 1933 forcing many of its highly talented members and associates into exile in different parts of the world. Some of them immigrated to Palestine and worked as architects and urban planners, notably on the construction of the new city of Tel Aviv. Tel Aviv's White City is a designated UNESCO World Heritage Site comprising around 4,000 buildings; as such it is the world's largest ensemble of modernist architecture and some of the buildings evince a pronounced Bauhaus influence in their overall design.

Many buildings today require refurbishment and restoration in keeping with the requirements of heritage conservation. The Federal Ministry is helping to fund the "Centre for the Conservation of Architectural Heritage in Tel Aviv's White City", which is due to open in September 2019 and will provide a focal point and concomitant network of expertise in support of conservation-minded building in the city. The project underlines the shared historical, architectural and cultural significance of the "White City" for both Germany and Israel alike. The focus of the German contribution is on the provision of technical expertise and strategies for heritage conservation.

The "White City Tel Aviv" initiative was also the springboard for the "Spring School Tel Aviv – 100 Years of the Bauhaus", the results and findings of which are compiled in this impressive catalogue. During 2018 and 2019, twenty-four students from Mainz, Braunschweig, Innsbruck and Jerusalem worked together in two workshops in Dessau and Tel Aviv respectively, undertaking an extensive examination of Bauhaus buildings in terms of their conception and construction; in the process they became acquainted with different approaches to the task of identifying and surveying the building stock, as well as receiving an opportunity to try out their own ideas.

The main objective of the project was fourfold: to raise the awareness of the participants about the issue of conservation-minded treatment of these listed buildings, to discover similarities between and peculiarities of the different regions, to investigate the conflict arising from the needs and standards of modern living on the one hand, and heritage concerns on the other, and ultimately to formulate solutions.

I would like to congratulate everyone involved for the successful completion and overall outcome of the project. I hope that by promoting the project we have been able to contribute, in a small but meaningful way, to the ongoing care of our architectural and cultural heritage, to intercultural understanding in general and to the friendship between Germany and Israel.

Berlin, May 2019

Anne Katrin Bohle
State Secretary
Ministry of the Interior, Building and Community

(next page) **The Liebling House in Tel Aviv, 2018, Photo: Yael Schmidt**

PREFIX
INTRODUCTION

Ultimately everything seems to come together almost of its own accord: assembling the team.

The project's inception dates back to 2011 when the Bezalel Academy of Arts and Design hosted a symposium on Erich Mendelsohn in Jerusalem. From that point on, Shmuel Groag, Architect and Conservation Consultant in Tel Aviv teaching at the Bezalel, and Regina Stephan, art historian and professor at the University of Applied Sciences in Mainz, shared an ardent desire to stage a joint workshop in which the students from these partner universities of many years standing might collaborate. The topic is obvious: the architecture of the modern movement in Israel as it exists in West Jerusalem, but particularly in Tel Aviv. Time passes, and in the meantime Regina Stephan had been appointed to the German-Israeli Advisory Board in her capacity as an expert on behalf of the Federal Ministry for the Environment, Nature Conservation, Building and Nuclear Safety (BMUB) which is involved in establishing and designing a Heritage Centre for the White City in Tel Aviv: the Liebling House. It is geared in particular towards informing both the general public about the White City's unique features and the experts about the structural and technical specifications of buildings in the International Style in Tel Aviv.

The idea of a joint German-Israeli student workshop met with tremendous support when Regina Stephan, in conjunction with Ulrich Knufinke, who was a visiting professor in the Institute of Architectural History at the University of Innsbruck at the time, presented their workshop concept in 2017: Movements of Modernism – The Architecture of Tel Aviv and its International Background. The first three of the team were now in position: Groag, Stephan and Knufinke.

The conference 100 Years of Planning and Building in Palestine and Israel (1918-2018) staged by Klaus Tragbar in April 2018 under the aegis of the Research Institute in the University of Innsbruck's Faculty of Architecture, supplied the final members of the team: Klaus Tragbar, Katrin Kessler from the Bet Tfila Research Unit for Jewish Architecture at the TU Braunschweig and Vladimir Levin, the director of the Center for Jewish Art at the Hebrew University of Jerusalem.

The concept of a joint workshop, begun in Innsbruck and further developed during a series of Skype conferences, led to the Director of the Bauhaus Dessau Foundation, Claudia Perren, also a member of the WCC Advisory Board, to suggest holding an open studio at the Bauhaus in Dessau to study original Bauhaus architecture in detail before the workshop in Tel Aviv and thus hone everyone's sensibilities for nuances in advance of the trip.

In the summer of 2018, the concept developed by Groag, Stephan, Knufinke, Tragbar, Kessler and Levin won over the support of Gunter Adler, Secretary of State responsible for the construction, housing and urban development sectors and who is now at the Federal Ministry of the Interior, Building and Community (BMI). At his instigation, the two-part workshop and its documentation in the form of an exhibition, catalogue and documentary film was granted sustained and generous funding from the Ministry and the Federal Institute for Research on Building, Urban Affairs and Spatial Development (BBSR) within the Federal Office for Building and Regional Planning (BBR). All

Participants of the workshop in Tel Aviv on Bialik Square, march 2019, Photo: Klaus Tragbar

the participants – the students and lecturers – are most grateful for this support. Without this funding the concept could not have been realised in this form.

Half of the quota of twenty-four students – all of them at an advanced stage of their degrees – came from the Bezalel Academy of Arts and Design and the TU Braunschweig, the University of Innsbruck and Mainz University of Applied Sciences. Numerous experts introduced them to and informed them about the Bauhaus in Dessau and modernist architecture in Tel Aviv and Jerusalem. All of the participants would like to thank the speakers and programme leaders most warmly:

Regina Bittner, Vincent Frank, Katja Klaus, Monika Markgraf, Werner Möller and especially Claudia Perren, Director of the Bauhaus Dessau Foundation, Director Shira Levy Benyemini and Programme Director Sharon Golan Yaron, WCC at the Liebling House, Tel Aviv, Zvi Efrat and Yuval Yaski of the Bezalel Academy of Arts and Design, Jersualem, Jeremie Hoffmann, Head of the Conservation Department, Municipality of Tel Aviv, Micha Levin, Shenkar-Ramat Gan, Lilach Harel and Shira Sprecher, architects, Tel Aviv. Special thanks are due to Yehudith Kiryati, Shmuel Mestechkin's niece.

It was the ministry's idea and initiative to document the workshop in a film. With Frithjof

Heinrich and Malte Röthig two young documentary film-makers joined the team. Educated at the Hochschule Mainz they were supervised by Hartmut Jahn.

Timothy Connell from London translated and proofread the book.

One workshop has the habit of begetting another workshop. The largely intact, original built-in interior of an apartment in the Kiryati House, as well as the numerous unretrieved documents in the Municipal Archive of Tel Aviv, await detailed study.

We hope and intend to continue this extremely stimulating, exciting and productive examination of a shared architectural heritage in Germany and Israel. Indeed, there is still so much research to be undertaken in order to understand it better, and there is so much to study in order to conserve it for the future.

Mainz, May 2019

Regina Stephan

PREFIX
METHODOLOGY

Shmuel Mistechkin, Kiryati House, Tel Aviv, 1938-1940

When faced with the task of converting or extending an existing building, an architect is not only concerned with the overall functional and constructional conditions of the task in hand, or indeed the intentions of his client, all of which challenge his creativity, but also with the existing physical structure his predecessors passed on to him. He will have to think about how he might define his approach to the existing structure: Should he conform and adopt the given architectural language?

Should he adopt individual motifs, but vary them to make his intervention stand out?

Does he develop his own architectural language, which then enters into a kind of dialogue with the existing building?

Or does he design something that is completely independent of or even at variance with the building that ultimately merely shares a physical connection?

Whichever approach he finally decides upon from the brief adumbration listed above, his decision must always be predicated upon careful analysis and thorough knowledge of the structure in question.

We took these basic considerations as an opportunity to expose students to such tasks within the framework of the "Spring School Tel Aviv – 100 Years of the Bauhaus 1919-2019" workshop. To this end, two buildings in Tel Aviv-Jaffa were selected, both designed by Bauhaus graduates whose work is of particular interest in 2019 as the Bauhaus celebrates its centenary: Shmuel Mestechkin's Kiryati House built between 1938 to 1940 in a prominent location on the corner of Rothschild Boulevard and Habima Square and Hans-Hermann (Chanan) Frenkel's blood bank built between 1953 and 1956.

Both buildings were carefully analysed and the parameters of the original designs studied, taking into consideration the historical context of the buildings, the architects' design concepts, the constructional and technical possibilities and materials available to them. Impressions of both buildings and their respective urban environments were recorded in hand-drawn sketches, structural surveys, photographs and verbal descriptions. The aim was to observe from close quarters, record and process artistically the actual situation in and around the building

in question. These first impressions were then presented, evaluated and critiqued. Visits to municipal offices in Tel Aviv followed and the relevant building regulations were retrieved, studied and evaluated.

On this basis, brief designs were drawn up in a concentrated workshop, during which the students examined the extent to which the buildings can be renovated in keeping with heritage conservation yet adapted for the needs of modern living. The differences between the conceptual approaches deployed at the respective participating universities and colleges in dealing with historical buildings clearly emerged in the process.

But what also became apparent was the fact that the real and imminent threat of demolition of both Bauhaus alumni buildings is not only unnecessary and unsustainable, it also doesn't make sense as both buildings can, with a series of small, sometimes surprising measures, be adapted to suit the current situation they find themselves in, that is to say, to be fit for today's needs, demands and uses.

We would be delighted if we could persuade the owners and the general public about the importance of both buildings and their preservation. Because ultimately sensitive and considered treatment of existing building stock is still the most sustainable, economical and ecological of all available options.

And it preserves the history of a place for future generations.

Mainz, 5 May 2019

Shmuel Groag MSc, Bezazlel Academy of Arts and Design, Jerusalem
Dr. Katrin Keßler, Bet Tfila Research Unit for Jewish Architecture in Europe, Technische Universität Braunschweig
Dr. Ulrich Knufinke, Lower Saxony State Office for the Preservation of Cultural Heritage, Hannover
Dr. Vladimir Levin, Centre for Jewish Art Hebrew University, Jerusalem
Prof. Dr. Regina Stephan, Hochschule Mainz, University of Applied Sciences, Institute for Architecture
Prof. Dr. Klaus Tragbar, Universität Innsbruck, Institute for Architectural Theory and History

Hans-Hermann (Chanan) Frenkel, Blood Bank, Jaffa, 1953–1956

MORE THAN BAUHAUS

OPEN STUDIO
AT THE BAUHAUS DESSAU
FOUNDATION

REGINA STEPHAN

PRECURSORS AND CONTEMPORARIES OF THE BAUHAUS

The modern architecture that emerged during the Weimar period is inconceivable without precursors, indeed, pre-war architecture and ideas provided the rich and fertile soil upon which it could flourish. To name but a few: Joseph Maria Olbrich, Frank Lloyd Wright, Theodor Fischer, Peter Behrens, Henry van de Velde, Le Corbusier and Tony Garnier made crucial contributions to the New Building of the Weimar era.

In particular, the work of Joseph Maria Olbrich can be identified as the birth of modernism. Influenced by what he had seen during his studies in Sidi Bou Said, Olbrich transferred the cuboid, whitewashed architecture of North Africa to Europe and, with the construction of the Vienna Secession building in 1897-98, was the first to present a white cube and the suggestion of a flat roof. He was also the first to realise a new exhibition concept, namely at the exhibition of the Darmstadt Artists' Colony on the Mathilden-höhe in 1901 titled *Ein Dokument Deutscher Kunst* (A Document of German Art): permanently built, fully furnished dwellings, which could be inhabited after the exhibition had ended.

This so-called *Darmstädter Prinzip* (Darmstadt Principle) was subsequently revived in numerous exhibitions, such as at the *Weißenhofsiedlung* (Weissenhof estate) in Stuttgart in 1927 or at the Interbau in Berlin in 1957. Olbrich's wedding tower of 1908 is the first example of the use of horizontal ribbon windows that extend around the building's corners, as well as projecting single balconies, similar to those Walter Gropius used in 1926 at the Prellerhaus in Dessau.

Olbrich's ideas flourished at the Bauhaus in an altogether different way: he demanded in 1898: "We have to build a city, a whole city! ... at its centre, however ... a house of work, simultaneously a studio for artists and a workshop for craftsmen, where the artist always has the calming and orderly handcraft at his disposal, whereas the craftsman always has the liberating and purifying force of art, until they both grow into one person! "(1) The Bauhaus' inaugural manifesto published in 1919 states: "Architects, sculptors, painters – we must all return to craftsmanship! For there is no art such thing as an 'artist by profession'. There is no essential difference between the artist and the artisan ... so let us create a new guild of craftsmen free from the divisive class distinctions that sought to build a lofty barrier between craftsmen and artists!" (2)

Olbrich's visions were thus revisited and woven into the core philosophy of the Bauhaus; indeed, the combination of school, studio and artists' houses in Dessau also has its precursor in the shape of Olbrich's artist colony at Darmstadt's Mathildenhöhe.

After the First World War in 1918 and as a result of the new, burgeoning political system of democracy and the concomitant importance ascribed to the needs of a broader swathe of the populace, the development of architecture in Germany comprised a series of many – at times – overlapping strands: it was at once expressionistic, organic, constructivist, industrialised, rooted in its native land.

LOGGIA BEI DER MOS

SIDI BOU SAID

Künstlerkolonie Darmstadt.
Blick vom Ernst-Ludwigshaus.

Halle für Flächenkunst.

Kunstanstalt Lautz & Isenbeck, Darmstadt. C 13119

Haus Olbrich.   Haus Keller.   Haus Deiters.   Haus Habich.

Initially congregating in the architects' association *Zehnerring* in 1923, which subsequently became *Der Ring* in 1926, a maximum of twenty-seven architects at its height represented a type of architecture that stood for a new beginning, devoid of nostalgic references to traditional architectural forms, but also by no means a unified architectural language. Their number included Otto Bartning, Richard Döcker, Otto Haesler, Arthur Korn, Hans und Wassili Luckhardt, Ernst May, Erich Mendelsohn, Bernhard Pankok, Hans Poelzig, Adolf Rading, Hans Scharoun, Bruno and Max Taut, Heinrich Tessenow, and the directors associated with the Bauhaus, Walter Gropius and Ludwig Mies van der Rohe, as well as Bauhaus employees Adolf Meyer and Ludwig Hilberseimer, but not the second Bauhaus director, Hannes Meyer.

Die Glückertschen Häuser.   Haus Christiansen.

Darmstadt Artist's colony
Mathildenhöhe, Exhibition
A Document of German Art, 1901,
Postcard, Institut Mathildenhoehe,
Darmstadt

figure in terms of Palestine's modern architecture, Ita Heinze-Mühleib describing the effect of his architecture to be akin to hearing a "catchy tune". (3) Yet this combination can be found in numerous buildings in Tel Aviv. An example of this is the Engel House on Rothschild Boulevard, built by Ze'ev Rechter in 1934, which fuses elements of his architecture with the one of Le Corbusier.

In view of the relatively small number of actual Bauhaus students Myra Wahrhaftig identifies in her study (3) – she only names six architects – it must be said that Tel Aviv's White City is much more than Bauhaus. It is the crucible of 1920s' modernist architecture.

Annotations

(1) Quoted from Hermann Bahr, "Ein Dokument Deutscher Kunst", in *Bildung: Essays* (Leipzig, 1900), pp. 45-52, here p. 46. Cf. Sandra Wagner-Conzelmann, "'Eine Stadt müssen wir erbauen, eine ganze Stadt!' Siedlungsplanung im Werk von Joseph Maria Olbrich", in Regina Stephan and Ralf Beil eds, *Joseph Maria Olbrich 1867-1908, Architekt und Gestalter der frühen Moderne*, exh. cat. Mathildenhöhe Darmstadt (Ostfildern 2010), pp. 204-211, here p. 206 f.
(2) Manifest und Programm des Staatlichen Bauhauses zu Weimar, 1919, in: Jeannine Fiedler, Peter Feierabend, Bauhaus, Köln 1999, p.180f.

Over and above these architects, Le Corbusier, Mart Stam and J.J.P. Oud made important contributions to the development of modern architecture in Germany during the 1920s.

The sum of many contemporaneous modern currents was subsumed under the term New

Building. And it was precisely this sum of modern architecture that found its way to Palestine and was the creative force behind the extant buildings of Tel Aviv's so-called White City. Nobody spoke of Bauhaus architecture as a style in the 1920s.

Erich Mendelsohn was a particularly significant

Erich Mendelsohn, Silkstore Weichmann, Gleiwitz, 1922,
Erich Mendelsohn-Archiv, Kunstbibliothek, Staatliche Museen zu Berlin

In 1928 Le Corbusier´s semi-detached house in the Weissenhof estate served
as background for the advertisement of the Mercedes-Benz 8/38 PS Roadster,
built in the years 1926 to 1928, © Mercedes-Benz Classic

(3) Ita Heinze-Mühleib, *Erich Mendelsohn. Bauten und Projekte in Palästina (1934-1941)* (Munich, 1986), p. 329 and p. 331. Referring to Leopold Krakauer's Teltsch Hotel in Haifa, she quoted him as saying " Le Corbusier and I."

(4) Myra Warhaftig. *Sie legten den Grundstein. Leben und Wirken deutschsprachiger Architekten in Palästina 1918-1948* (Tübingen and Berlin, 1996). She cites Arieh Sharon, Edgar Hed (Hecht), Chanan Frenkel, Shlomo Bernstein, Shmuel Mestechkin and Munio Gitai (Weinraub).

Ze´ev Rechter, Engel House
on Rothschild Boulevard, 1933,
Photo: Regina Stephan, 2019

REGINA STEPHAN

ARCHITECTURE AT THE BAUHAUS
Curriculum and practice 1919-1933

The new school's name says it all: Bauhaus. The medieval word "Bauhütte" (Church masons' guild) also resonates here – that collective of artists, artisans and craftsmen who collaborated as a closely-knit group on the construction of the cathedrals creating the given magnum opus as a collective, concerted effort. Now, centuries later, the building itself should be "the ultimate goal of all artistic activity". "Architects, painters and sculptors," wrote the Bauhaus' founding director, Walter Gropius, "must learn a new way of seeing and understanding the composite character of the building, both as a totality and as a sum of its parts. Their work must then reimbue itself with the spirit of architecture, which is lost in salon art." (1) The Bauhaus "strives to bring together all creative effort into one whole, to reunify all the disciplines of practical art - sculpture, painting, handicrafts, and the crafts – as inseparable components of a new architecture." (2) It wanted "to educate architects, painters, and sculptors of all levels, according to their capabilities, to become competent craftsmen or independent creative artists and to form a working community of leading and future

artist-craftsmen. These kindred spirits, will know how to design buildings harmoniously in their entirety – structure, finishing, ornamentation, and furnishing." (3)

The concept of the early Bauhaus was the total departure from all degree studies at academies, universities and polytechnic colleges. The job titles that were chosen for the members of the Bauhaus made this abundantly clear: with a leaning towards craftsmanship, the students were called apprentices, journeymen and young masters, the teachers were known as masters and as a body, a Meisterrat or Masters' Council. "The manner of the teaching arises from the nature of the workshop." (4) As was the custom until the end of the eighteenth century, an architect would learn his craft from a master in order to become a master builder himself.

The system of teaching at the Bauhaus, itself a reflection of these ideas, is illustrated by the six-month-long preliminary course at the beginning of the apprenticeship, i.e. the study of elementary form and materials in the so-called pre-workshop. This was followed by a three-year course in core subjects, such as materials, colour

and form, and above all the apprenticeship in the glass, clay, stone, wood, metal, fabric and paint workshops. Only after this three-and-a-half-year or seven-semester-long course of study did the students arrive at construction per se. The degree was to be a certificate of apprenticeship issued by the Chamber of Trades and Crafts and "if necessary, the Bauhaus". (5)

The actual teaching of building from the eighth semester onward included "practical involvement in building (on actual construction sites related to Bauhaus projects) and free training in building (on the Bauhaus trial site) for particularly capable apprentices." (6) This teaching was intended to lead to a "master craftsman's certificate, issued by the Chamber of Trades and Crafts and if necessary, the Bauhaus".

Presented in 1923, the Haus am Horn dwelling was one of the first State Bauhaus showcases in Weimar, inasmuch as its architecture and its rich interior were designed and manufactured by the young master, Georg Muche and other graduates of the school respectively, all of whom had progressed through the Bauhaus programme.

Das Endziel aller bildnerischen Tätigkeit ist der Bau! Ihn zu schmücken war einst die vornehmste Aufgabe der bildenden Künste, sie waren unablösliche Bestandteile der großen Baukunst. Heute stehen sie in selbstgenügsamer Eigenheit, aus der sie erst wieder erlöst werden können durch bewußtes Mit- und Ineinanderwirken aller Werkleute untereinander. Architekten, Maler und Bildhauer müssen die vielgliedrige Gestalt des Baues in seiner Gesamtheit und in seinen Teilen wieder kennen und begreifen lernen, dann werden sich von selbst ihre Werke wieder mit architektonischem Geiste füllen, den sie in der Salonkunst verloren.

Die alten Kunstschulen vermochten diese Einheit nicht zu erzeugen, wie sollten sie auch, da Kunst nicht lehrbar ist. Sie müssen wieder in der Werkstatt aufgehen. Diese nur zeichnende und malende Welt der Musterzeichner und Kunstgewerbler muß endlich wieder eine bauende werden. Wenn der junge Mensch, der Liebe zur bildnerischen Tätigkeit in sich verspürt, wieder wie einst seine Bahn damit beginnt, ein Handwerk zu erlernen, so bleibt der unproduktive „Künstler" künftig nicht mehr zu unvollkommener Kunstübung verdammt, denn seine Fertigkeit bleibt nun dem Handwerk erhalten, wo er Vortreffliches zu leisten vermag.

Architekten, Bildhauer, Maler, wir alle müssen zum Handwerk zurück! Denn es gibt keine „Kunst von Beruf". Es gibt keinen Wesensunterschied zwischen dem Künstler und dem Handwerker. Der Künstler ist eine Steigerung des Handwerkers. Gnade des Himmels läßt in seltenen Lichtmomenten, die jenseits seines Wollens stehen, unbewußt Kunst aus dem Werk seiner Hand erblühen, die Grundlage des Werkmäßigen aber ist unerläßlich für jeden Künstler. Dort ist der Urquell des schöpferischen Gestaltens.

Bilden wir also eine neue Zunft der Handwerker ohne die klassentrennende Anmaßung, die eine hochmütige Mauer zwischen Handwerkern und Künstlern errichten wollte! Wollen, erdenken, erschaffen wir gemeinsam den neuen Bau der Zukunft, der alles in einer Gestalt sein wird: Architektur und Plastik und Malerei, der aus Millionen Händen der Handwerker einst gen Himmel steigen wird als kristallenes Sinnbild eines neuen kommenden Glaubens.

WALTER GROPIUS.

Bauhaus Manifesto.
Left page: Lyonel Feininger,
Woodcut 1919,
© VG Bildkunst

(next page also:)
Text by Walter Gropius

PROGRAMM

DES

STAATLICHEN BAUHAUSES
IN WEIMAR

Das Staatliche Bauhaus in Weimar ist durch Vereinigung der ehemaligen Großherzoglich Sächsischen Hochschule für bildende Kunst mit der ehemaligen Großherzoglich Sächsischen Kunstgewerbeschule unter Neuangliederung einer Abteilung für Baukunst entstanden.

Ziele des Bauhauses.

Das Bauhaus erstrebt die Sammlung alles künstlerischen Schaffens zur Einheit, die Wiedervereinigung aller werkkünstlerischen Disziplinen — Bildhauerei, Malerei, Kunstgewerbe und Handwerk — zu einer neuen Baukunst als deren unablösliche Bestandteile. Das letzte, wenn auch ferne Ziel des Bauhauses ist das Einheitskunstwerk — der große Bau —, in dem es keine Grenze gibt zwischen monumentaler und dekorativer Kunst.

Das Bauhaus will Architekten, Maler und Bildhauer aller Grade je nach ihren Fähigkeiten zu tüchtigen Handwerkern oder selbständig schaffenden Künstlern erziehen und eine Arbeitsgemeinschaft führender und werdender Werkkünstler gründen, die Bauwerke in ihrer Gesamtheit — Rohbau, Ausbau, Ausschmückung und Einrichtung — aus gleich geartetem Geist heraus einheitlich zu gestalten weiß.

Grundsätze des Bauhauses.

Kunst entsteht oberhalb aller Methoden, sie ist an sich nicht lehrbar, wohl aber das Handwerk. Architekten, Maler, Bildhauer sind Handwerker im Ursinn des Wortes, deshalb wird als unerläßliche Grundlage für alles bildnerische Schaffen die gründliche handwerkliche Ausbildung aller Studierenden in Werkstätten und auf Probier- und Werkplätzen gefordert. Die eigenen Werkstätten sollen allmählich ausgebaut, mit fremden Werkstätten Lehrverträge abgeschlossen werden.

Die Schule ist die Dienerin der Werkstatt, sie wird eines Tages in ihr aufgehen. Deshalb nicht Lehrer und Schüler im Bauhaus, sondern Meister, Gesellen und Lehrlinge.

Die Art der Lehre entspringt dem Wesen der Werkstatt:

Organisches Gestalten aus handwerklichem Können entwickelt.

Vermeidung alles Starren; Bevorzugung des Schöpferischen; Freiheit der Individualität, aber strenges Studium.

Zunftgemäße Meister- und Gesellenproben vor dem Meisterrat des Bauhauses oder vor fremden Meistern.

Mitarbeit der Studierenden an den Arbeiten der Meister.

Auftragvermittlung auch an Studierende.

Gemeinsame Planung umfangreicher utopischer Bauentwürfe — Volksund Kultbauten — mit weitgestecktem Ziel. Mitarbeit aller Meister und Studierenden — Architekten, Maler, Bildhauer — an diesen Entwürfen mit dem Ziel allmählicher Einklang aller zum Bau gehörigen Glieder und Teile.

Ständige Fühlung mit Führern der Handwerke und Industrien im Lande.

Fühlung mit dem öffentlichen Leben, mit dem Volke durch Ausstellungen und andere Veranstaltungen.

Neue Versuche im Ausstellungswesen zur Lösung des Problems, Bild und Plastik im architektonischen Rahmen zu zeigen.

Pflege freundschaftlichen Verkehrs zwischen Meistern und Studierenden außerhalb der Arbeit; dabei Theater, Vorträge, Dichtkunst, Musik, Kostümfeste. Aufbau eines heiteren Zeremoniells bei diesen Zusammenkünften.

Umfang der Lehre.

Die Lehre im Bauhaus umfaßt alle praktischen und wissenschaftlichen Gebiete des bildnerischen Schaffens.

A. Baukunst,
B. Malerei,
C. Bildhauerei

einschließlich aller handwerklichen Zweiggebiete.

Die Studierenden werden sowol handwerklich (1) wie zeichnerisch-malerisch (2) und wissenschaftlich-theoretisch (3) ausgebildet.

1. Die handwerkliche Ausbildung — sei es in eigenen allmählich zu ergänzenden, oder fremden durch Lehrvertrag verpflichteten Werkstätten — erstreckt sich auf:

a) Bildhauer, Steinmetzen, Stukkatüre, Holzbildhauer, Keramiker, Gipsgießer,
b) Schmiede, Schlosser, Gießer, Dreher,
c) Tischler,
d) Dekorationsmaler, Glasmaler, Mosaiker, Emallöre,
e) Radierer, Holzschneider, Lithographen, Kunstdrucker, Ziselöre,
f) Weber.

Die handwerkliche Ausbildung bildet das Fundament der Lehre im Bauhaus. Jeder Studierende soll ein Handwerk erlernen.

2. Die zeichnerische und malerische Ausbildung erstreckt sich auf:

a) Freies Skizzieren aus dem Gedächtnis und der Fantasie,
b) Zeichnen und Malen nach Köpfen, Akten und Tieren,
c) Zeichnen und Malen von Landschaften, Figuren, Pflanzen und Stilleben,
d) Komponieren,
e) Ausführen von Wandbildern, Tafelbildern und Bilderschreinen,
f) Entwerfen von Ornamenten,
g) Schriftzeichnen,
h) Konstruktions- und Projektionszeichnen,
i) Entwerfen von Außen-, Garten- und Innenarchitekturen,
k) Entwerfen von Möbeln und Gebrauchsgegenständen.

3. Die wissenschaftlich-theoretische Ausbildung erstreckt sich auf:

a) Kunstgeschichte — nicht im Sinne von Stilgeschichte vorgetragen, sondern zur lebendigen Erkenntnis historischer Arbeitsweisen und Techniken,
b) Materialkunde,
c) Anatomie — am lebenden Modell,
d) physikalische und chemische Farbenlehre,
e) rationelles Malverfahren,
f) Grundbegriffe von Buchführung, Vertragsabschlüssen, Verdingungen,
g) allgemein interessante Einzelvorträge aus allen Gebieten der Kunst und Wissenschaft.

Einteilung der Lehre.

Die Ausbildung ist in drei Lehrgänge eingeteilt:

I. Lehrgang für Lehrlinge,
II. „ „ Gesellen,
III. „ „ Jungmeister.

Die Einzelausbildung bleibt dem Ermessen der einzelnen Meister im Rahmen des allgemeinen Programms und des in jedem Semester neu aufzustellenden Arbeitsverteilungsplanes überlassen.

Um den Studierenden eine möglichst vielseitige, umfassende technische und künstlerische Ausbildung zuteil werden zu lassen, wird der Arbeitsverteilungsplan zeitlich so eingeteilt, daß jeder angehende Architekt, Maler oder Bildhauer auch an einem Teil der anderen Lehrgänge teilnehmen kann.

Aufnahme.

Aufgenommen wird jede unbescholtene Person ohne Rücksicht auf Alter und Geschlecht, deren Vorbildung vom Meisterrat des Bauhauses als ausreichend erachtet wird, und soweit es der Raum zuläßt. Das Lehrgeld beträgt jährlich 180 Mark (es soll mit steigendem Verdienst des Bauhauses allmählich ganz verschwinden). Außerdem ist eine einmalige Aufnahmegebühr von 20 Mark zu zahlen. Ausländer zahlen den doppelten Betrag. Anfragen sind an das Sekretariat des Staatlichen Bauhauses in Weimar zu richten.

APRIL 1919.

Die Leitung des
Staatlichen Bauhauses in Weimar:
Walter Gropius.

Teaching scheme of the Bauhaus,
published in the statues of the Bauhaus,
1922, translated by Frederick van Amstel

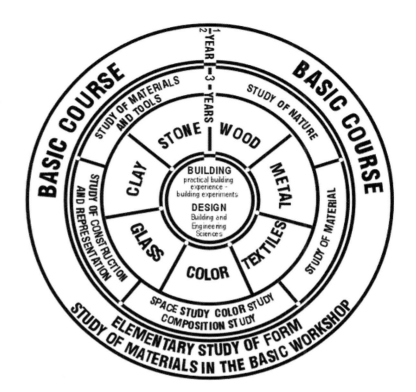

The holistic approach deployed in the Haus am Horn is particularly interesting: the house was designed for a family of three or four, all of its interiors were fully furnished and equipped with all the necessities for daily life.

Gropius used this first Bauhaus exhibition to develop Olbrich's Darmstadt Principle from 1901. It was based upon the idea of presenting fully-furnished houses with a design concept built to last. The aim in both cases was to present a comprehensive vision for new, contemporary living to the general public.

As was the case in Darmstadt, the construction of the experimental house in 1923 was "the beginning of cooperation with industry geared toward to exploring … the challenges facing new housing and new technical possibilities leading to the gradual implementation of the results." (7) For Gropius, it showed the "dependence of such building entities on industry and the economy."(8) Thus, after the first study cycle at the Bauhaus had been completed, the emphasis of the course shifted from handcraft to industry. In 1923, Gropius expressed his hope that the graduates "will

co-opt machines in the service of their ideas," and that "industry … will seek out and use their all-round training". (9) During the years that followed prior to the move to Dessau, Gropius focussed on the relationship between industry and handcrafts. Two years later he saw them in a state of "constant convergence", and even classed handcraft as a "vehicle for experiment for and toward industrial production". (10)

In the mid-1920s, the focus of the Bauhaus shifted increasingly toward industry and thus to rationalisation within the construction sector. This was also apparent from a design point of view with the construction of the new school building in Dessau. Gropius justified the complete departure from the early Bauhaus doctrine and the first Bauhaus buildings, such as the Sommerfeld House from 1920/21 and the development of the

other buildings in Dessau, as follows: "propelled by the tremendous housing shortage, the technical and creative forces of the people are turning to the new developments in construction." (11) Industry played a key role in this process.

The Bauhaus relocated to the new school building in Dessau in 1926, the masters moved into their appointed masters' houses. Having been officially afforded the status of a Design College, the Bauhaus masters were appointed to the rank of professor.

The Törten housing estate, designed by Gropius between 1926 and 1928 and comprising small terraced houses, was intended to alleviate the noticeable housing shortage in Dessau. The houses were made of industrially-fabricated components and, as such, were commensurate with the shift in focus of the Bauhaus as well as a general trend in building. This trend is also exemplified by the Frankfurt estates, which were built by Ernst May up until 1930, who had been appointed city councillor and municipal building surveyor in 1925.

When Gropius resigned from the post of director on 3 February 1928, he was followed by a specialist in the construction of mass housing, Hannes Meyer, who had been in charge of the architecture department for almost a year. Meyer made incisive and permanent changes to course: he subdivided the architecture department in "a. construction and b. interior design". This is particularly noteworthy because the officially-established building department had only very few students. According to Martin Kieren, there were "never more than ten students per semester who studied architecture at the Bauhaus or completed the building course." (12) Meyer shifted the emphasis of the Bauhaus' work in favour of architecture, resulting in the other workshops being more or less obliged to subordinate, adapt and channel their work toward architecture. In 1928, he said that he was "extremely keen to obtain a commission with our building department". (13) Under Meyer, the teaching was restructured: the workshops became "a kind of production works" in which the students were required, on three days of the week, to spend eight hours per day on workshop projects that pursued the demand for the "needs of the people instead of the needs of luxury". (14) On two other days, a day

of "science" and a day of artistic activities made up the timetable.

Between 1929 and 1930, Meyer supplemented Gropius' recently-built estate in Törten with trellised residential buildings – apartment blocks with ninety rented flats for workers and lower-ranking employees. If the houses in Gropius' estate represented a widely affordable option for homeowners, Meyer now backed the concept of the so-called Volkswohnung or people's flat. Realised during the years of the severe global economic crisis and hardship, they are symptomatic of the changed focus of the Bauhaus. This shift in focus was also reflected from 1929 onward in the increase in the number of politically and ideologically-inflected lectures. (15) Meyer's ultimate goal was to "release the Bauhaus from its role as a provider of a style" and return it "more to nature, the social environment and the people in order that it might have a right to exist." (16) Meyer's Marxist sympathies, reflected in ideological and thematic bias of the lectures and tolerance of Communist activity at the School, ultimately led to his dismissal as director in 1930.

Ludwig Mies van der Rohe succeeded Meyer to become the third director of the Bauhaus. After the success of the Werkbund exhibition "The Apartment" in Stuttgart in 1927 with his Weissenhof estate, also based on the Darmstädter Prinzip (Darmstadt Principle), as well as his German Pavilion at the 1929 Barcelona International Exposition, he had reached the pinnacle of his fame. At the Bauhaus, he restructured the subject bau/ausbau or building / extending. (16)

Although no detailed curriculum has survived, conclusions can be drawn about the six-semester study programme from the diplomas issued at the time. It was now much more in keeping with a classical architecture degree: basic subjects such as descriptive geometry, mathematics and norms of science were taught in the first semester, continued in the second and third semester and supplemented by design and construction, structural engineering, domestic engineering, et cetera. More complex building challenges followed in the fourth semester, such as urban and housing development, the construction of housing estates, as well as a "purely aesthetic training in individual housing". The course was designed to last of six semesters and thereby corresponded to the duration of a standard Bachelor's degree today. It is interesting that attendance at the Municipal Building College in Dessau was recommended for specialist topics not covered by the Bauhaus course. The influence of teachers, such as Ludwig Hilberseimer, who taught at the Bauhaus from 1929 until 1933, is unmistakable in students' work.

With the Nazis making up the strongest fraction in the Dessau Town council after the elections in November 1931, the situation for the Bauhaus became increasingly parlous, and ultimately the continuation of operations in Dessau became impossible. Almost a year later in October 1932, "bauhaus berlin" opened under Mies van der Rohe's direction in a telephone factory in Berlin-Steglitz. It had as many as on hundred and sixty-eight enrolled students for the summer semester of 1932, including thirty-three foreign students. (17). Among them were the students Shmuel Mestechkin and Chanan Frenkel, who, after returning to Mandatory Palestine, transferred Bauhaus ideas and

philosophy to their work there, as indeed did Arieh Sharon, who had studied at the Bauhaus from 1927 until 1931.

After a period of fourteen years and four months, Mies van der Rohe, effectively the Institution's last director, dissolved the Bauhaus on 20 July 1933 because he was unable to meet the conditions for its continued existence laid down by the Nazi authorities. Its closure went largely unnoticed in professional circles, both nationally and internationally. (18) However, Bauhaus teachers and alumni continued to disseminate its ideas, teaching and fame across the world.

Annotations

(1)   Walter Gropius, "Programm des Staatlichen Bauhauses in Weimar" in Jeannine Fiedler and Peter Feierabend, eds, Bauhaus (Cologne, 1999), p. 180.

(2)   Walter Gropius, Fiedler/Feierabend, Bauhaus, p. 181.

(3)   Walter Gropius, Fiedler/Feierabend, Bauhaus, p. 181.

(4)   Walter Gropius, Fiedler/Feierabend, Bauhaus, p. 181.

(5)   Walter Gropius, Idee und Aufbau des Staatlichen Bauhauses Weimar (Munich, Weimar: Bauhausverlag, 1923), quoted from: Hartmut Probst, Christian Schädlich, Walter Gropius. Ausgewählte Schriften, vol. 3 (Berlin, 1987), p. 86.

(6)   Walter Gropius, Idee und Aufbau, p. 91.

(7)   Walter Gropius, Idee und Aufbau, p. 91.

(8)   Walter Gropius, Idee und Aufbau, p. 91.

(9)   Walter Gropius, Idee und Aufbau, p. 91.

(10) Walter Gropius, "Grundsätze der Bauhausproduktion", in Neue Arbeiten der Bauhaus-Werkstätten, Bauhausbücher 7 (Munich, no year) (1925), pp. 5-8 quoted from: Probst/Schädlich, Ausgewählte Schriften, p. 93f., here p. 94.

(11) Walter Gropius, "glasbau", in Die Bauzeitung, 12, 1926, 20, S. 159-162, quoted from: Probst/Schädlich, Ausgewählte Schriften, pp. 103-106, here p. 103.

(12) Martin Kieren, "Das Bauhaus auf dem Weg zu einer Produktivgenossenschaft – der Direktor Hannes Meyer", in Fiedler/Feierabend, Bauhaus, pp. 204-215, here: p. 207.

(13) Martin Kieren, "Das Bauhaus auf dem Weg", p. 209f.

(14) Martin Kieren, "Das Bauhaus auf dem Weg", pp. 210-211.

(15) Martin Kieren, "Das Bauhaus auf dem Weg", p. 213.

(16) All references from Bauhaus Archive, ed., Der vorbildliche Architekt. Mies van der Rohe. Architekturunterricht 1930-1958 am Bauhaus und in Chicago, exh. cat. Bauhaus-Archiv Museum für Gestaltung (Berlin, 1986), p. 57.

(17) For the dates, please cf.: https://www.bauhaus-bookshelf.org/chronik_chronologie_1919_1933.html. Last accessed 2 May 2019.

(18) The result of research undertaken by Elmar Kossel on contemporary Italian architecture magazines Domus, Architettura e Arti decorative, Casabella as well as the art journal Emporium via, Institute of Building History at the University Innsbruck. The lecture "Die Multiple Moderne" held at the University of Innsbruck in January 2019 under the auspices of International Day of Study will be published in the conference journal due to appear at the end of 2019.

MONIKA MARKGRAF

CONSERVATION CHALLENGES AND SOLUTIONS AT THE BAUHAUS IN DESSAU

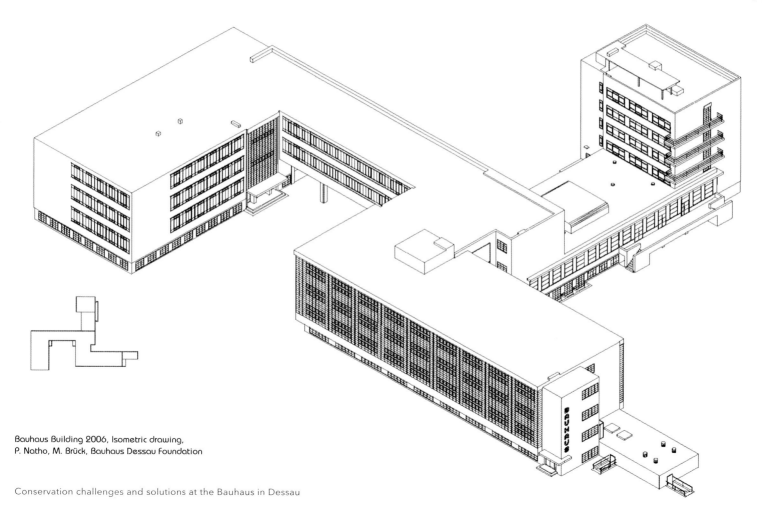

Bauhaus Building 2006, Isometric drawing,
P. Natho, M. Brück, Bauhaus Dessau Foundation

Main entrance to the
Bauhaus Building,
Bauhaus Dessau
Foundation, Photo:
Christian Irrgang, 2012

The Bauhaus building in Dessau was built in 1926 according to Walter Gropius' plans and is considered a key work for the development of modern architecture in Europe at the beginning of the twentieth century. It combines the principles of functionalism with an extraordinary architectural quality and is characterised by the use of modern materials for the time, such as glass, steel and reinforced concrete. The Bauhaus building was added to the UNESCO list of World Heritage Sites in 1996 and is now used by the Bauhaus Dessau Foundation for its artistic and academic operations. (1)

An overall historical monument preservation objective was devised detailing the building works necessary for the long-term conservation of the building. (2) It is a comprehensive concept in which the different aspects and concerns were analysed and evaluated in context. This guideline includes basic requirements, such as minimalising the number of modifications to the physical substance of the building. Provision is made for sections of and structural components within the building depending on whether restoration or reconstruction, repair, maintenance or remoulding is the objective. (3) The development and updating of the objective is a joint endeavour involving the close cooperation between the relevant parties, viz. the Bauhaus Foundation as a user and owner, the research/building archaeology department at the Bauhaus Foundation and specialist planners. With regard to conservation and heritage interests, the responsibility lies with the Lower Dessau Office for Heritage, the Regional Conservation and Heritage Authority and the International Council on Monuments and Sites (ICOMOS).

The specifications for the steel and glass façades exemplifies this differentiated approach. The Bauhaus building's large windows not only serve a practical function, but their transparency and reflective surfaces define the character and aesthetic of this kind of architecture. Owing to the expanse of glass surfaces and concomitant significant loss of energy, the Bauhaus Dessau Foundation has devised a complex concept for reducing energy loss while at the same time safeguarding the cultural values of the building, combining changes in use with innovative technical solutions.

The following specifications have been made for the conservation of the windows: the period windows are being preserved and restored. Windows reconstructed in 1976 with modified profiling and simplified opening mechanisms will be repaired and replaced only in selected areas by windows with thermally insulated profiles and double-glazing. Windows in areas that retain the look of the architecture or are important for historical reasons remain single-glazed. All windows will be painted white on the inside and grey on the outside according to the period model. The needs of energy conservation are met via differentiated analysis and evaluation, the traces of alterations to the façades remain visible so that at the same time the original, unique architectural quality of the building with its glass façades can be fully appreciated. (4)

Annotations

(1) www.bauhaus-dessau.de
(2) Arge Bauhaus, Brambach and Ebert, Halle/Saale and Pfister Schiess Tropeano, Zurich: General historical monument preservation objective Bauhaus Dessau (Dessau, 1999); ProDenkmal, Bamberg and Berlin: update of conservation aims, Dessau 2014. Unpublished document, Bauhaus Dessau Foundation.
(3) Cf. Monika Markgraf, ed., *Archeology of Modernity. Renovation Bauhaus Dessau* (Berlin, 2006).
(4) Cf. Monika Markgraf, "The Glass façades of the Bauhaus Dessau Building", in Franz Graf, Francesca Albani, eds, *The Glass in the 20th century Architecture: Preservation and Restoration / Il vetro nell'architettura del XX secolo: conservazione e restauro* (Mendrisio, 2011). Academy of Architecture – Università della Svizzera italiana.

WEST

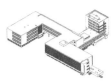

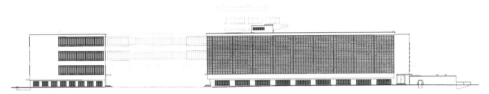

Elevation West

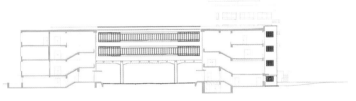

Elevation West and Cross Section

Elevation Prellerhouse

Western glas surface areas of the Bauhaus Building in Dessau,
Conservation objective, 2014, Bauhaus Dessau foundation
(Denkmalpflegerische Zielstellung 2014, 2, p 1)

NORTH

Elevation North 1

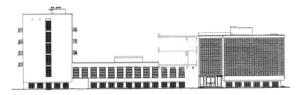

Elevation North 2

LEGEND

Windows 1926
▪ Preservation

Windows 1976
▪ Preservation
▪ Energetic renewal check
▪ Transformation possible

Windows 2006 – Reconstruction after original
▪ Preservation
▪ Energetic renewal check
▪ Transformation possible

Windows 2012
▪ Energetic renewal executed

Northern glas surface areas of the Bauhaus Building in Dessau,
Conservation objective, 2014, Bauhaus Dessau foundation
(Denkmalpflegerische Zielstellung 2014, 2, p 2)

Authenticity and Modernity: The remaining wall of the original Gropius' House and the house's reduced modern rebuilding by Bruno Fioretti Marquez, 2014. The way the windows are positioned in the facade and the opaque glass distinguish the building from the original.
Photo: Regina Stephan, 2018

Dessau Törten Housing Estate, Terraced houses and Konsum Building on the right side after completion 1928, Aerial View Junkers, Hauptstaatsarchiv Nordrhein-Westfalen, RW 229-27331

MONIKA MARKGRAF

THE DESSAU-TÖRTEN HOUSING ESTATE AND ITS CONSERVATION

The Dessau-Törten housing estate was built between 1926 and 1928 as a Bauhaus experiment in residential housing. According to Walter Gropius' plans, 314 detached dwellings were to be built in three sections with the aim of creating widely affordable housing via a rationalisation and industrialisation of the building process. The types of houses, which Gropius called "Sietö", differed in construction, floor plan and elevation and fittings. The façades facing the street of the two-storey terraced houses had an individual architectural quality due to the arrangement of white, plastered surfaces, horizontal steel ribbon window as well as other features. (1)

Adaptations were made over the decades by the owners of the dwellings (which were always privately owned) to meet their changing needs. Examples of the alterations include reinforcement and redesign of the thin outer walls, replacement of the steel ribbon windows with wooden punched windows, replacement of Luxfer prism glass in concrete frames with simple windows in other places, or enlargement of the living space by means of garden extensions. On the one hand, the alterations derive from deficits in

Dessau Törten Housing Estate, Terraced houses, Bauhaus Dessau Foundation, Photo: Nils Emde, 2012

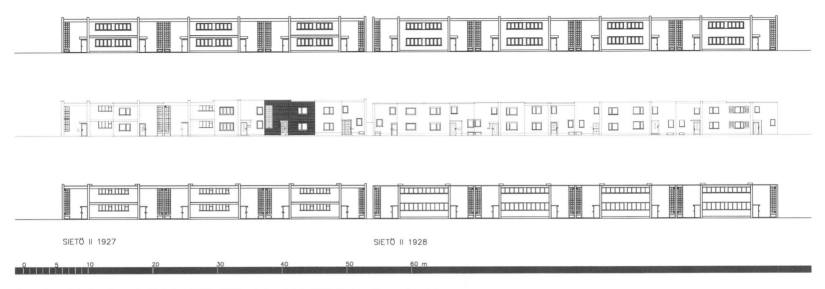

SIETÖ II 1927   SIETÖ II 1928

0   5   10   20   30   40   50   60 m

Comparison of the facades to the Kleinring, 1928 – 2000 – design statute 1994, Bauhaus Dessau Foundation

the original planning or implementation, and on the other, they reflect a shift in owners' tastes, preferences and standards. As a result of these changes, the original architectural quality disappeared.

The estate was listed as an urban conservation site within the district of Halle in 1977. This marks a turning point in the appreciation of Bauhaus architecture. Prospective renovations were subject henceforward to a so-called conservation consultation. At the beginning of the 1990s, the pressure for change also increased due in part to the almost unlimited availability of new building materials. The city passed a design statute in 1994 that no longer permitted radical modifications to the original architecture, such as the cladding of exterior brickwork. Guidelines have been established for the shades of the façades, the proportions and layout of the windows and other features. However, the requirements of the design statute did not correspond to the original appearance of the houses, representing instead a compromise between the original design and the needs of the residents. In addition, scientifically-sound analysis of this architecture did not exist in 1994.

Today, twenty-five years on from the enactment of the design statutes, renovations have been carried out on a large number of these houses in keeping with these specifications.

Almost 100 years left their traces: uniform façades have been changed to non-uniform, Bauhaus Dessau Foundation, Photo: Martin Brück, 2010

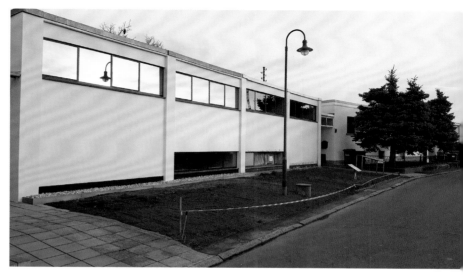

A sample for the entire Housing estate: reconstructed façade, Bauhaus Dessau Foundation, Photo: Monika Markgraf, 2019

Thus, neither the original design with its clear structure and typification, nor the individual wishes of the residents have shaped the image of the estate, as a third variant has been created in accordance with the guidelines of the directive – which can be misinterpreted as original Bauhaus design. (2)

A further development has emerged in recent years: as a result of the growing appreciation of Bauhaus architecture, individual owners have become interested in the restoration of original features, such as the façades. The conservation of the estate's design, enshrined in the design statute preventing radical alterations that might disfigure the buildings, is thus enjoying an increasing upturn in the form of the restoration of individual façades, giving rise in turn to a differentiated picture.

Annotations

(1) Cf. Andreas Schwarting, *The Settlement Dessau Törten. Rationalization as an aesthetic program* (Dresden, 2010).

(2) Cf. Reinhard Matz and Andreas Schwarting, eds, *The Disappearance of the Revolution in Renovation. The History of the Gropius Settlement Dessau-Törten* (1926-2011) (Berlin, 2011).

The Dessau-Törten housing estate and its conservation

SHMUEL GROAG
DESSAU-TÖRTEN INTERVENTIONS

Photographs, first sketches
and renderings made during the Dessau
workshop, Bauhaus Dessau Foundation,
Photo: Nathalie Wächter, 2018

The workshop in Dessau gave us the opportunity to demonstrate in a very short period of time the essence of the conservation studio methodology we have been using at Bezalel over the past ten years, whereby interventions in heritage sites are utilised as a catalyst to discuss the problems and update conservation discourse in terms of the ongoing progress in standards.

This pedagogical attitude of an open-minded restructuring of knowledge takes its lead from some of the Bauhaus teaching ideas. The main principle of the intervention is based on current conservation charters as presented in the Burra Charter and theory (1). The emphasis is moving from "material-led conservation" to "value-led conservation" (2). Common to both approaches is the fact that the act of conservation itself is not just focussed on the material subject of the building; other social and cultural values of the site are equally important in the interventions.

The main goal of the exercise was to produce interventions based on the given site's cultural significance recognised by the students following a professional tour and historically-themed lecture that preceded it.

The first exercise was aimed at defining some aspects of the cultural significance of the Dessau-Törten dwelling and to produce an open impression on the site without using architectural tools. Analysing the results together enabled the whole group to understand the special values and phenomena of the site.

The second exercise focused on options for additions to and extension of conservation stock. After a lecture on additions ethics and supporting examples, the students were divided into four mixed groups of six students per group. Each group was tasked with a different type of intervention:

- restoring the site to its original design
- additions to/extensions of the original stock and techniques used
- additions/extensions that differ from/contrast with existing architectural elements
- an addition or extension using a ultra-modern techniques

The results were discussed within the larger forum and revealed a great variety of creative solutions that challenge the conservative approach of normal conservation practice.

Today, the Bauhaus site is facing a typical problem in the field of cultural heritage. The Bauhaus in Dessau – which, more than any other school of architecture in the world and for the best part of a century, has embodied the endeavour to liberate the architect's creative spirit through a practice of change, disassembly and reassembly of every object – has become a site of strictly-monitored conservation in which no single element can be changed. The Bauhaus of the Weimar era was not restricted by the preservation of the past and encouraged new interventions and creative thinking. Its approach guided us in the Dessau workshop and opened up options for the students to produce challenging results in a short period of time.

Annotations

(1) Meredith Walker and Peter Marquis-Kyle, "The Illustrated Burra Charter: Good Practise for Heritage Places", Cultural Heritage Centre for Asia and the Pacific, Burwood, Australia ICOMOS Inc, 2004.

(2) Munoz Vinas, Salvador, Contemporary Theory of Conservation, Amsterdam, 2008.

THE STUDENT´S WORKS

TÖRTEN – PROJECT 1: ADDITION USING EXISTING MATERIALS – DESSAU TÖRTEN SIETÖ II

Sophie Gumpold, Paulina Knodel, Chen Gabay, Maya Nissan

ANALYSIS

Sietö II is a terraced housing development. Consequently all units are the same in themselves – apart from being mirrored and then tacked together in a row. Each unit consists of two halves, which are slightly displaced in relation to one another. When viewed from the street, the ensuing aspect of the façade – comprising alternating projections and recesses – could effectively be continued ad infinitum. The site map shows that there is a triangular-shaped green space at the end of each street. All in all there are seven such areas. They have no specific or designated function and are otherwise used by the residents of the estate.

IDEA

The main idea of these green spaces in the design is to give the streets a recognisable 'end'. Using the existing materials from Sietö II, another unit is added at the end of the road that enhances the green space. The cubature of the terraced houses is to be maintained, but the materials are to be used differently than they are in the existing stock. The glass bricks, for example, take the place of the outer walls in this unit, whereas the windows remain completely open. This creates a transparent, open and minimalistic complement to the terraced houses, which can simultaneously be identified as contemporary and yet it still sets itself apart from the rest of the street.

USE

During the inspection of the estate we noticed that there were hardly any pedestrians out and about, let alone children. Therefore, we decided to turn the supplementary buildings into a meeting place for the neighbourhood – especially as a communal play area geared towards learning. The aspect of the street façade continues but behind there is an open space. The original separation into rooms within the building is rendered visible on the ground by markings and some low walls that serve as seating. The playground is equipped with the so-called Törten Lego, a collection of toys based on the architectural elements of the Gropius buildings. Thus, an awareness of and sensitivity to the Dessau-Törten estate and its history is generated in both young and older generations alike.

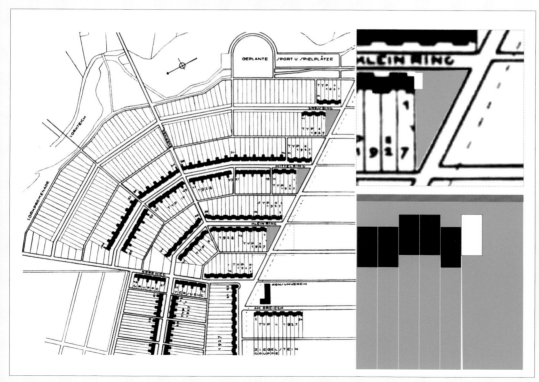

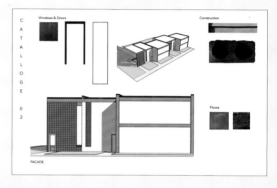

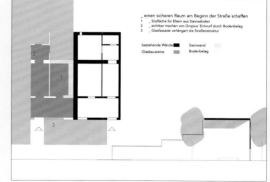

1927

1998

2018

2018

FUTURE

Törten – Project 2: Parasite

Quynh Huong Ngo, Arne Müchler,
Sharon Pery, Leopold Walther

A parasite needs a habitat, a residue upon which
it can establish itself and use to develop itself.

ANALYSIS

During the analysis of the master plan, three
incisive elements were singled out that give the
estate its geometry and structure. They are situated in the centre of the estate.

SQUARE

As the first recognisable centre, Gropius placed
the Konsum cooperative building at the intersection of the main axes of the estate.

CIRCLE

Gropius underlined his confidence in the
modern age and its technical possibilities by
positioning the electricity pylon centrally. It towers
above the estate just like the church over the
village in earlier times.

TRIANGLE

The main axis: Damaschke Straße and the
Nordweg form a central square next to the
electricity pylon and the Konsum building, Törten
residents' former grocery store.

INTERVENTION

As the most important element, a glass sphere was positioned on the single-storey part of the Konsum building, which limits the space like a kind of stage. It sits enthroned on the Konsum building, which it uses parasitically as a host for its own mis en scène. At the same time, however, it also enters into a form of symbiosis with it, as its bold gesturality adopts the formal idiom of the Bauhaus, accentuating it and thus giving it even more force. Ultimately, what emerges is an intervention that harnesses formal language of the ensemble and then stages it through bold gestures.

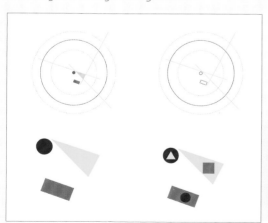

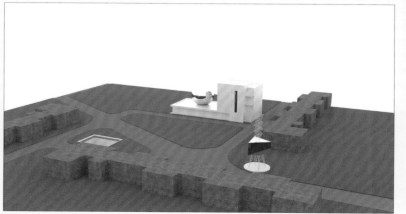

TÖRTEN – PROJECT 3: BOXES

Marlon Dina, Marius Druyen, Nohar Hochberg, Maria Korpachev

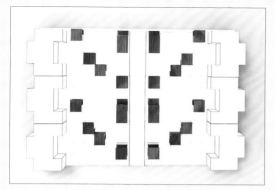

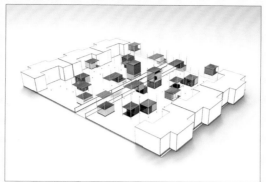

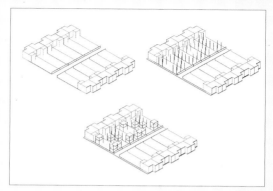

The design was based on the idea of supplementing the existing housing stock of the development using a new material that is unusual for Törten. The first consideration here was where and in what way could such an extension come about. The individual plots have large gardens, which were used as vegetable gardens during the construction period. The gardens are no longer used in the same way and today have largely been grassed over with lawns.

Since the design should serve as a kind of catalogue for the residents so that they can extend their properties in keeping with their personal needs, a grid was placed over the garden to accommodate individual uses. In simply constructed boxes that sit on stands, space is converted and scope created for storage, workshop and hobby needs. The intention of the project is to give the residents a guideline to best accommodate their needs qualitatively and to reactivate the unused area.

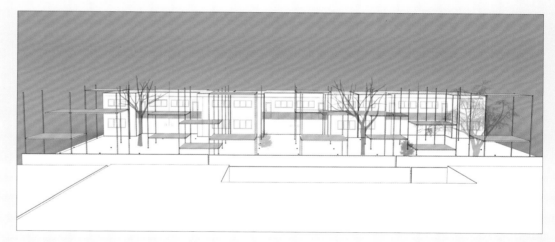

In addition, reversibility and a low environmental footprint were important considerations. Owing to the fact that residents' needs can change over time, it must be possible to supplement and dismantle the system as the case may be.

The construction consisting of wooden posts and point foundations ensures this degree of flexibility and also the quick installation, addition and removal of subsystems.

TÖRTEN – PROJECT 4: MODERN LIVING IN AN OLD SHELL

Shir Sara Moallem, Nelly Panchenko

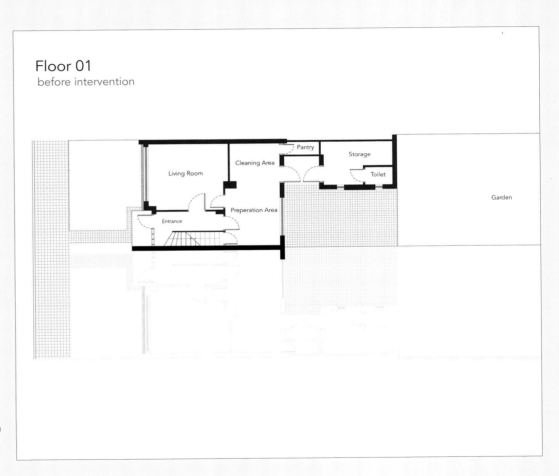

Floor 01
before intervention

Pantry

Storage

Cleaning Area

Living Room

Toilet

Garden

Preperation Area

Entrance

The floor plans of the terraced houses in Dessau-Törten no longer correspond to today's inhabitant's desires for permeability and flowing space. In addition, the band of windows placed by Gropius just underneath the ceiling was in practice perceived by many residents as sitting too high. Therefore they have often been replaced by windows that sit at a conventional height in the facade. However, this massively changed the appearance and unity of the row of terraced house.

The aim of this design consequently was to install modern, flowing spaces for living behind a facade according to Gropius' design. A 44 cm high pedestal at the window allows the residents to enjoy the view despite the windows installed in their original position.

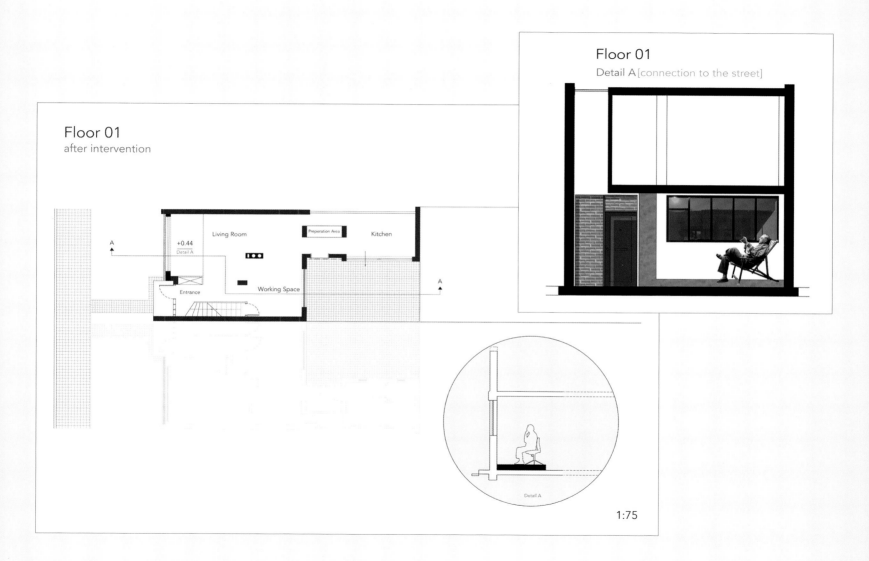

Floor 01
after intervention

A
+0.44
Detail A

Living Room

Preperation Area

Kitchen

Entrance

Working Space

A

Floor 01
Detail A [connection to the street]

Detail A

1:75

MORE THAN BAUHAUS

SPRING SCHOOL
TEL AVIV

ULRICH KNUFINKE

A MELTING POT OF MODERNITY

International architecture in Tel Aviv and Jerusalem before the founding of Israel

Planning and building in Palestine during the British Mandate between 1920 and 1948 is characterised by divergent developments – yet, in the shape of Tel Aviv's "White City" and Jerusalem's New City, it produced two extraordinarily extensive and, stylistically-speaking, surprisingly uniform cityscapes in modern architecture during the 1930s that are almost without compare worldwide.

In spite of all the differences between modern Jerusalem, which developed from the end of the nineteenth century onward mostly to the west of the old city, and Tel Aviv, which was founded in 1909 as a garden suburb just outside the old port Jaffa, both cities share the distinction of having been planned to a great extent by architects who had not grown up in the country. The internationality of the architects (not to mention their clients), with their differing educational backgrounds and individual architectural signatures, was an essential ingredient of the

(left) Alexander Baerwald,
Technion, Haifa, Postcard 1934, Private Collection

modernist flux on the eastern shores of the Mediterranean during that era.

However, since the nineteenth century, when Palestine was still part of the Ottoman Empire, the "Holy Land" once again became the focus of European powers. In keeping with their colonial self-image, European superpowers saw themselves as the champions and guardians of Christianity: to be visible here in the holy site of salvation legitimised and inflated their own hegemonic claims. Building Christian, ecclesiastical institutions in Jerusalem, Bethlehem and

elsewhere was a demonstration of political interests that no European superpower was prepared to forgo – and in the age of historicism, with its invention of national styles, it was obvious that architecture had to be formulated as a kind of emblem of national tradition and claim to that very cultural and political hegemony. Jerusalem in particular was occupied with monuments of a characteristically European (French, British, Russian, German, Italian) and North American flavour until the time of the Mandate. The architectural landscape of Palestine was quintessen-

Friedmann and Rubin, Jeshurun Synagoge Jerusalem,
Photo: Ulrich Knufinke, 2017

Erich Mendelsohn, Anglo Palestine Bank Jerusalem,
Photo: Ulrich Knufinke, 2019
(prevoious pages)

(left) Friedmann and Rubin,
Apartment house, Photo: Ulrich Knufinke, 2019

tially international (not unlike world expositions
with their collections of national pavilions), but
paradoxically there was an absence of actual
international architecture.

Against a different background, another group
from Europe pursued the goal of a national
architecture in the Promised Land: Jews, who,
under the auspices of Zionism, immigrated from
the beginning of the twentieth century onward
in order to realise the idea of a national Jewish
identity in the "Old New Land". The establishment of the first Jewish art academy, the Bezalel
Academy in Jerusalem (founded in 1906), and
the Technion (Israel Institute of Technology) in
Haifa as a college for engineering and architecture (planning commenced in 1909, first in-take
of students followed in 1924) were milestones
on this journey. It was here that artists and
architects trained in Europe sought a new
"Hebrew" style based on a concept of national
identity, which should be appropriate for the
new Jewish people and their surroundings in
the Middle East. Well-known examples, such
as Josef Barsky's Herzliya Grammar School
(1909) in Tel Aviv, Alexander Baerwald's

Technion Building in Haifa (1912) or Yehoshua
Zvi Tabachnik's Diskin Orphanage in Jerusalem
(1924) bear witness to the experiments geared
toward embellishing local oriental forms with
Jewish Hebrew symbolism (and simultaneously
combining them with European traditions).
The eclectic villas and homes of the older parts
of Tel Aviv exemplify the betimes awkward
handling of these forms in everyday architecture.

When Jewish settlement received official
support from the British government by virtue
of the Balfour Declaration of 1917, the structures were already in place in which the body
of Jewish settlers (Yishuv) could flourish in
new cities, such as Tel Aviv or new cooperative
agricultural settlements (kibbutzim, moschawim),
and create its own architecture. This development was viewed from Europe both euphorically
and critically, the transfer of ideas taking place
in an atmosphere of intensive mutual exchange
between the Yishuv and Europe. The fact that
Jews from Palestine attended the Bauhaus in
Dessau at the end of the 1920s to study state-
of-the-art planning, design and construction is
only one aspect of this exchange.

Friedmann and Rubin,
Apartment house,
Staircase, Photo:
Ulrich Knufinke, 2019

Wilhelm Zeev Haller,
residential building, Ben Yehuda Str 230,
Municipality of Tel Aviv, Building Archive

(right page) Apartment building Jaffa,
1930s, Photo: Ulrich Knufinke, 2019

Tel Aviv street scenery, early 1930s,
from: Annie Mainz, Das ist Tel Aviv,
published 1934

In terms of their respective infrastructures,
both the New City of Jerusalem and Tel Aviv
were developed into modern cities during the
1920s – Jerusalem as the site of the Mandate
Government and the antecedent Jewish adminis-
tration with its proto-status as capital, Tel Aviv as
a bourgeois garden suburb (or rather: suburban
garden) of multi-religious and ethnic Jaffa, which
in turn experienced a push to modernise and
underwent a significant number of expansions.
Two decisions for what are now wholly different
cityscapes were made in the early years of the
British Mandate: the decree demanding that
all buildings in Jerusalem should be dressed
with local limestone out of respect for the old
town, and that the planning of Tel Aviv should

adhere to the concept for the city put forward by the Scottish pioneering town planner, Patrick Geddes in 1925, which envisioned a green "garden city" cooled by the sea breezes and replete with avenues and detached houses. In the early 1930s, the decision was also made to build in the European modernist style with bright, plaster façades free from ornament and with flat roofs: the modern age was to be henceforward the hallmark of the new Jewish community and settlement.

The movement towards modern architecture as a "style" of building in Palestine was precipitated by the inevitable demise of the German Weimar Republic and the Nazis' subsequent seizure of power and the beginning of what would be a reign of systematic persecution, disenfranchisement and expropriation of Jews. Palestine was one of many possible destinations for Jewish immigrants, but here they were to have special influence as architects, planners and builders.

Upon arrival, the German-Jewish immigrants encountered a Jewish society, which was itself of international origin. In addition to German-trained architects, there were professionals from France, Belgium, Great Britain, Poland, Czechoslovakia, Hungary, Austria or the Soviet Union all working in the veritable melting pot that was Palestine at the time. Teaching carried out at German universities, such as Berlin-Charlottenburg, Munich or Darmstadt and "New Building" as a concept played a prominent role here, inasmuch as German modernism was universally considered to be at the vanguard of developments in the field. The Bauhaus was biographically important to some architects in Palestine, but its importance should not be overestimated given the rich genealogy of modernism. Hans Poelzig, Adolf Loos, Henry van de Velde, Le Corbusier or Erich Mendelsohn were by far more important as teachers and architects for Palestine (and elsewhere) than the Dessau school. Perhaps the omnipresent link between Israeli modernism and Bauhaus doctrine can only be traced back to the clever self-marketing of Arieh Sharon – student of Gropius and Hannes Meyer and later head of the state planning authority – who laconically titled his complete works Kibbutz und Bauhaus.

The construction boom in Tel Aviv's White City and Jerusalem's New City, which has produced such memorable modernist structures in plaster and limestone, was short-lived. It ground to a halt in the late-1930s as a result of the burgeoning civil tensions between the resident and Jewish populations, which threatened to escalate into outright war, coupled with outbreak of the Second World War itself at the end of the decade. The establishment of Israel in 1948 marked the beginning of a new phase of planning and construction in the region, which would however have been completely unthinkable without the remarkable "melting pot" era during the 1920s and 30s. The universal "victory march" of the International Style during the interwar period had actually begun here a decade earlier, producing unique ensembles, such as Tel Aviv's White City and Jerusalem's New Town.

SHMUEL GROAG

URBAN PLANNING OF JAFFA
pre-1948 and three conservation plans afterwards

Modern urban development in Jaffa had already begun in the final years of the Ottoman Empire and not just – as is generally assumed – during the British Mandate. Analysis of maps and aerial photographs of Jaffa at the close of the Ottoman era indicates that various areas throughout the city had already undergone a measure of urban development. New neighbourhoods, such as Ajami, Jabeliya, Neve Tzedek and Ahuzat Bayit (the core of Tel-Aviv), had been established on the periphery of Jaffa, effectively enabling the Arab and Jewish upper-middle classes to move out of the Old City. The development of new neighbourhoods was based on private initiatives, transforming agricultural plots into suburban areas. Controlled by the government and the municipality, this process was slow and organic, devoid of formal regulatory planning. A fascinating synergy obtained in pre-1948 Jaffa between built-up urban areas and the citrus orchards around and within the city. The combination of orange orchards and built-up areas gave Jaffa – quasi synonymous with the fruit – its "City of Oranges" moniker, the felicitous scent of citrus blossoms intermingling with the aroma of everyday urban life.

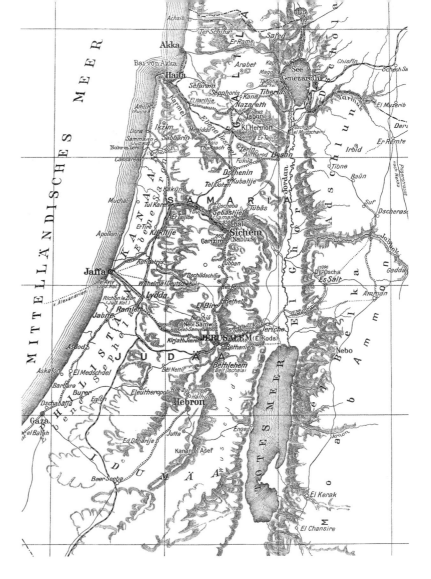

Map of Palestine, 1925, from: Ludwig Preiss, Paul Rohrbach, Palästina und das Ostjordanland, Stuttgart 1925, p. 231

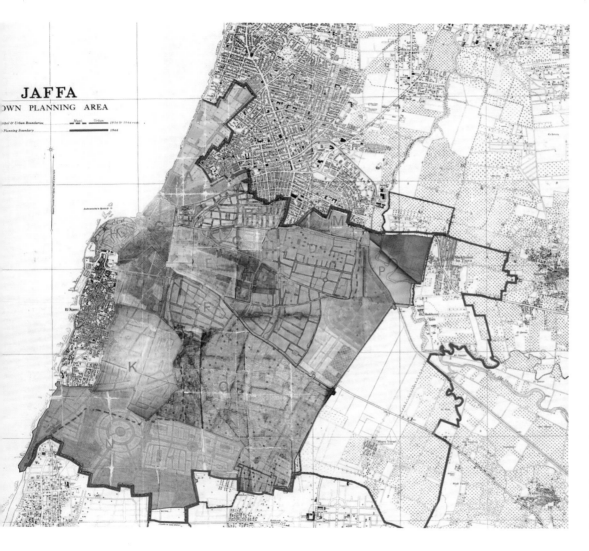

JAFFA

OWN PLANNING AREA

Compilation of the 15 detailed plans for Jaffa till 1948,
Groag Harel architects

BRITISH PLANNING –
HENRY KENDALL THE COLONIAL TOWN PLANNER

Statutory planning was one of the tools developed by the British Mandate imported into Palestine and other colonies. Jaffa topped a priority list of cities "in need of city planning". (2), as early as October 1920 prior to the establishment of the Central Planning Committee in Jerusalem. The attempt of the Mandatory government to work together with the Palestinian local authorities met with suspicion, distrust and even resistance.

Patrick Geddes, the renowned Scottish town planner, who was also commissioned to design a plan for Jaffa to accompany his design for Tel Aviv, claimed that his reason for not including Jaffa in the overall strategy was that – unlike the full cooperation he enjoyed from his Tel Aviv colleagues – the Jaffa city engineer, Hannah Salem was unwilling to cooperate. (3) This uncooperative attitude may well be interpreted as a reaction to the British professional liaison with the planners of Tel Aviv, which was part of what can be described as a "double colonial" system, a practice that

Aerial view of Jaffa 1932, Matson collection

ultimately turned Jaffa into an enclave, both physically and in terms of planning.

Geddes was succeeded by Clifford Holiday – the protégé of the renowned British architect and town planner, Patrick Abercrombie – and became the first head of the Central Planning Committee. Holiday drew up a master plan for Jaffa (the map of which is lost). Based on this master plan, Kendall and his team subsequently developed and approved fifteen detailed subsidiary plans.

Henry Kendall (1903-1983), the government planner in Palestine between 1936-1948, was the son of the British Engineer General in India (4). Kendall studied architecture at University College London and was appointed to the post in Palestine, by the Colonial Office at the age of thirty-two after service in Malaysia. Kendall's career in Palestine began just before the Great Arab Revolt and continued for thirteen years almost until the end of the British Mandate in 1948. As the official town planning advisor to the

government, Kendall worked in Jaffa, Haifa, Tel Aviv, Tiberias, Nablus, Be'er Sheva and Gaza, and his department grew from just five staff members in 1936 to no fewer than fifty by the late-1940s. However, a comparative analysis of the fifteen detailed plans for Jaffa, reveals a lack of urban vision. In many areas, the plans appear to be a regularisation of the existing urban fabric

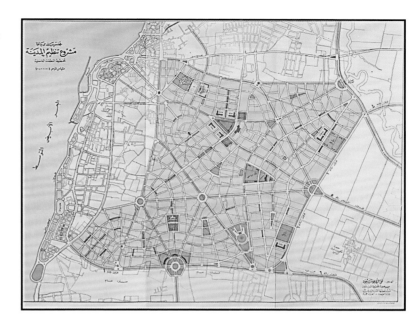

The Ali El Maligi Massoud
plan 1946, National
Library Jerusalem

stemming from local landowners' initiatives. Some plans (chiefly Plan N) were influenced by the popular "garden cities" trend in planning.

A moment of crisis for Jaffa and civil planning followed the Arab Revolt of 1936. As a measure to suppress the revolt and inflict punitive reprisals, the British authorities destroyed the heart of the Old City, which was shaped like an anchor. (5) The so-called "Anchor Plan" was explained as a strategy to "improve the Old City". This military-controlled, punitive act cleared the way for Henry Kendall's Plan H, a totally new and modern version for the historic Old City.

NEW JAFFA, LOCAL MODERNISM – THE ALI AL-MALIJI MASSUD PLAN

In 1946, Yousef Haikal, the last mayor of Jaffa, asked the Egyptian prime minister for help in the promotion of planning and improvement of Jaffa, its decrepitude drawing both internal and external criticism. Two professionals were recruited for this enterprise: Ali al-Maligy Massoud, "the father of Egyptian urban planning" (6), and the architect Ottoman Rafi Roustom.

Massoud, born in 1898, received his engineering qualification from the Ecole Polytechnique in Cairo in 1924. Parallel to the New Jaffa project, Massoud planned the workers' city of Imbaba near Cairo, characterised by liberal planning concepts. Massoud was also one of the founders of the Majalat Al-Imarah, an innovative journal of architecture and urban planning, published in Cairo between 1939 and 1959.

The "Jaffa Planning Project" (7) envisioned a Jaffa of the future as the economic and cultural capital of Palestine and a regional Arab centre, in keeping with the general spirit of progress in the world at the time. The plan sought to create change in the urban shape of Jaffa and to double the built area of the city. The plan outlined the development of a new extension to Jaffa to the south in the sand dunes between Bat Yam and Holon, as well as another new "Sand City" in the Nabi Rubin area. In order to connect Jaffa to this putative "Sand City" of the future, an access route was required in the 600-meter-long corridor between Bat Yam and Holon.

This bottleneck in the dunes became the centre of a political and legal wrangle. The Arab Higher Committee addressed the High Commissioner of Palestine, requesting the expansion of Jaffa's municipal area toward the sand dunes.

Their main arguments related to the fact that Jaffa's expansion had already been impeded by the development of Tel Aviv from the north and further development to the east would be at the expense of orchards and the lands of neighbouring villages. This complaint reflected the fact that the British authorities had extended the boundaries of Tel Aviv to the north and the east, including village lands, as in the case of the villages of Sumeiil and Sheikh Muwanis. While Tel Aviv was enlarged by some 6,000 dunams, Jaffa's municipal area was only enlarged by 200 dunams.

SEPARATION, DETACHMENT AND ANNEXATION

The pressure to detach Jewish neighbourhoods, such as Florentine and Neve Sha'anan, from Jaffa, together with its encirclement by Jewish towns from the outside, was outlined in the partition plan (1947), as Jaffa remained an Arab enclave at the heart of the proposed Jewish state. Its inferior strategic position was one of the factors that led to the rapid conquest of Jaffa and its surrender on 14 May 1948, leading to the displacement of more than 70,000 Jaffa citizens to Gaza among other places.

After the surrender of Jaffa, as few as 3,400 Palestinians remained in the city, which had been placed under martial law (subsequently revoked in 1949). Jaffa was annexed by Tel Aviv in 1950 and became again a vibrant metropolis once more with the arrival of more than 50,000 Jewish immigrants, mostly from the Balkans, who occupied the empty houses of the displaced Palestinian populace. Those houses, shops and land were confiscated by the state under the "Absentee Property Law" in 1950.

The town plans drawn up during the British Mandate period were abandoned in the early 1960s. Later in the decade, new "modern Euro-centric" town planning schemes were approved by the Tel-Aviv-Jaffa municipality earmarking many of the historic urban areas for demolition and structural renewal in the spirit of the modern movement. It wasn't until the late 1980s that new conservation-oriented plans were approved by the "Jaffa Planning Team" under a wholly different dispensation.

CONSERVATION PLANS

Conservation plans for Jaffa after 1948 can be divided in three phases. During the first decade of the State of Israel, two major neighbour-hoods in Jaffa were demolished: the Manshiya neighbourhood along the seashore and the Old City of Jaffa. While Manshiya – most of which is covered today by Charles Clore Park – was totally destroyed, an informed, professional debate about the economic benefits of heritage through tourism, effectively saved the buildings in front of the harbour sea front. (8)

At the beginning of the 1960s, a new approach was developed as the Old City area was designated an "architectonic reserve" and the site was restored as an "artist village" in one of Israel's first conservation plans. The street names were renamed after the signs of the zodiac, supressing every vestige of their Palestinian heritage.

In the mid-1980s and after more destruction of hundreds of houses in the historic neighbour-hoods of Ajami and Gabeliya, the Tel Aviv-Yafo municipality changed its policy and created the "Jaffa Team". The "Jaffa Team" published a guide to the Ajami quarter using analysis of the existing architectural typologies as a model for future buildings. New pieces of town planning promoted by the team encouraged developers to renovate surviving buildings, even if they were not listed as conservation sites.

Nowadays, Jaffa is under intense pressure from the real estate boom in Tel Aviv and a vigorous gentrification process. Both threaten to erase the memory of pre-1948 Jaffa and displace more Palestinian citizens, this time at the behest of neoliberal economics. The fact that Jaffa is not part of Tel Aviv's conservation plan and that the conservation policy is limited to a small number of listed buildings, highlights anew the urgent need to draw up an integrated and professional conservation plan for one of the oldest towns in Israel.

Annotations

(1) This paper is based on an article in preparation under titled "New Jaffa – Planning Modernity during the British Mandate Period from Henry Kendall to Ali Massoud" (working title).

(2) Hyman Benjamin, "British Planners in Palestine, 1918-1936", A Thesis submitted for the degree of Ph.D. The London School of Economics and Political Science, 1994.

(3) Hyman 1994.

(4) Lapidot Abraham, "Regional Planning during the British Mandate", Seminar at the Geography Department, Hebrew University Jerusalem, 1977.

(5) Gavish Dov, ‚The Old City of Jaffa, 1936. A colonial urban renewal project'."Eretz-Israel 17, 66-73, 1984.

(6) Mercedes Volait, "Architectes et Architectures de l'Égypte Moderne", 1830-1950 genèse et essor d'une expertise locale (Maisonneuve et Larose, 2005).

(7) Massoud Ali al-Maligy, "Jaffa Planning Project", in Karim, Sayyid, ed. Majallat al-Imarah 6-7-8 (Cairo, 1949).

(8) Yair Paz, "Conservation of the architectural heritage of abandoned urban neighborhoods following the War of Independence", Cathedra 88: 95–134, 1998. In Hebrew.

(9) Daniel Monterescu, and Roy Fabian, "'The Golden Cage': Gentrification and Globalization in the Andromeda Hill Project, Jaffa". Theory and Criticism 23, 141-178, 2003.

ELÉNA HINSCH
BAUHAUS ALUMNI IN TEL AVIV

Among the immigrants to Palestine seeking protection from Nazi persecution were twenty-five Bauhaus-trained architects and artists. Many, like Heinz Schwerin or Ricarda Meltzer, came to the country "due to the absence of other options", but as far as the four architects who worked in Tel Aviv were concerned, their Zionist convictions were instrumental. (1) They already lived in Palestine in the 1920s and designedly went for their studies to the Bauhaus in Dessau. Afterwards they just returned to the emerging city of Tel Aviv.

For Bauhaus members, Dessau was merely an induction into the International Style. They returned to Tel Aviv. Because of the spread of Zionist movements, Palestine had already established itself as destination for Jewish immigration since the 1880s and so the desire for the first Jewish city united the lives and careers of these four men.

ARIEH SHARON, who was born in 1900 in Jaroslau as Ludwig Kurzmann, immigrated in 1920 and was a founder member of the Gan Shmuel kibbutz. His first architectural designs were so forward-looking that the kibbutz gave him a sabbatical for a year in Germany in 1926. In 1927 he was one of the first students in the newly-established building department at the Bauhaus, which was run by Hannes Meyer. Sharon later worked in his office at the ADGB in Bernau. But he did not follow Meyer to Moscow when the latter lost his job at the Bauhaus, returning instead to Tel Aviv to build it as a modern city. His buildings, such as the Meonot Ovdim, are a defining example of the "New Building" concept and the integration of architecture and urban planning. But he also retained a connection to the kibbutz movement. He designed a total of five kibbutz plans for the movement.

CHANAN FRENKEL followed a similar path. Born in Halle, as a young man he travelled with the Fourth Aliyah to Palestine and helped to build the Givat Brenner kibbutz in 1928. He came to Germany three years after Arieh Sharon to study at the Bauhaus and graduated in 1932. Back in Tel Aviv, he worked in various architectural firms and on behalf of the British Army in Iraq. His delicate health and his premature death at the age of fifty-two restricted his output, whereby the blood bank in Jaffa is one of his most impressive works.

Also **SHLOMO BERNSTEIN** was born in Lithuania and went to study with a Zionist youth movement in Mandatory Palestine. At first he participated in the general building up of the country but subsequently decided to study in Haifa with Alexander Baerwald, with whom he enjoyed a close friendship. Indeed, Baerwald was the person who advised him to study at the Bauhaus, which Bernstein put into practice in 1931 becoming a dedicated disciple of Mies van der Rohe during his time there. After completing his studies in Dessau in 1932, he moved to Paris to gain further experience in Le Corbusier's studio. He returned to Tel Aviv in 1933 and – before moving into construction management on account of his health – built functional residential buildings, such as his renowned apartment buildings.

While Arieh Sharon, Chanan Frenkel and Shlomo Bernstein left for Palestine as a result of personal commitment to Zionism, fifteen-year-old **SHMUEL MESTECHKIN** was still too young to make such a decision. He travelled to Palestine with his parents in the Third Aliyah. Mestechkin attended the Bauhaus in the same year as Bernstein, as he was unable to take up a place in Haifa because he hadn't taken his baccalaureate. The closure of the Bauhaus in 1933 effectively curtailed his studies and prompted his eventual return to Tel Aviv to set up his own architectural office. In addition to residential buildings, such as the Kiryati House, he used his education mainly for the design of development plans for over sixty kibbutzim. At all times adhering to the Bauhaus principle, his unerring credo was "simplicity and care in the proportions and forms of expression." (2)

These four architects were a conduit for the teaching of the Bauhaus, which flowed with abundance into the architectural design of Tel Aviv. The impressions from Germany, combined with influences from architects and sponsors from different countries of origin, the dictates of the prevailing climatic conditions notwithstanding, created a unique architectural aesthetic known today as the "White City".

Annotations

(1) From Ricarda Schwerin's letter to Hannes Meyer dated 4 March 1948. Deutsches Architekturmuseum, Estate Hannes Meyer, quoted from: Ines Sonder, Werner Möller, Ruwen Egri, Vom Bauhaus nach Palästina. Chanan Frenkel, Ricarda und Heinz Schwerin, Bauhaus-Taschenbuch Nr. 6, Leipzig 2013, S. 108.

(2) Quoted from: Bar-Or, Galia et al., Kibbutz und Bauhaus. Pioniere des Kollektivs, exh. cat., Bauhaus Dessau (Leipzig, 2012), p. 48. The eponymous exhibition ran from 24 November 2011 until 28 May 2012.

SHARON GOLAN-YARON

CONSERVATION IN TEL AVIV TODAY – CONSERVATION POLICY

Tel Aviv was declared a UNESCO World Heritage Site in 2003 due to its outstanding cultural significance resulting from the wealth of extant examples of so-called "New Building" and town planning in the early twentieth century. It is considered to be the largest urban concentration of the early International Style. All in all, there are 3,700 International Style buildings in Tel Aviv, 1,000 of which were selected for conservation. One hundred and eighty buildings have been listed with a high grade of protection.

The UNESCO declaration led to the implementation of a Conservation Plan devised for the purpose of restoring the built fabric of the city. The starting point for the plan was the need for the city to continue growing while at the same time striving to preserve its historical heart. Most buildings in the city are privately owned, the conservation regulations are designed to enable residents to afford the relatively high price of the restoration and conservation process by granting additional building rights on the rooftops of listed buildings – revenues from the additional areas cover the cost of renovation. In practice, building rights can allow up to three storeys to an existing building, depending on criteria specific to each site. On top of the owners' obligation to renovate the building according to strict conservation regulations, they are also obliged to reinforce the building against earthquakes and add a missile shelter. As Tel Aviv is located on the Syro-African rift, it faces the prospect of potentially massive seismic activity threatening many of its buildings. The granting of additional construction rights is conditional upon the reinforcement of existing structures, preparing and protecting them from this eventuality.

Another reason for reinforcement is the constant threat of missile attack. To protect civilians, each individual apartment receives an additional reinforced missile shelter, preferably in form of a shaft in the rear of the building that cannot be seen from the front. The two predominant conservation challenges are: protection against natural disasters and finding ways to promote positive heritage mentalities.

Naturally, some conservation purists may raise an eyebrow at this "topping up" process, yet the municipality of Tel Aviv is bravely resisting enormous pressure from real estate giants by rele-gating the construction of high-rise buildings to areas lying outside the listed zones. It is paying a high price for trying to conserve its historical centre: investors are suing the municipality for 2.5 billion US-Dollars as compensation for loss in real estate value.

When planning the building extensions, the architect's task is anything but straightforward. The architect has to bear in mind that immense importance was attached to the proportions of modernist architecture. Some of the buildings have been extended by up to three additional storeys, sometimes doubling the overall height of the structure in the process.

If the extension has been built in the same style as the original building, the delicate horizontal proportions are in danger in view of the compromised proportionality of the original. Imitating the original style would also make it impossible to distinguish between the original building and its new extension. If, on the other hand, all new extensions are designed in a different architectural style, this novel "upper city" would soon dominate and overwhelm the historical buildings on the lower storeys. Since

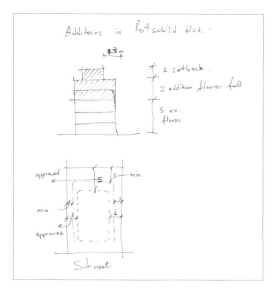

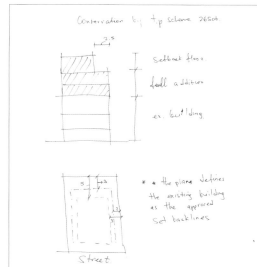

(left) **Building Rights by town planning Scheme,**
Groag Harel Architects

(right) **Building Rights in Rothschild**
Boulevard, Groag Harel Architects

(bottom) **The same house restored and extended on the left**
and original and aged on the right, Photo: Eléna Hinsch, 2019

every building in Tel Aviv has its unique character, the original proportions of the building must be carefully analysed as well as its particular position on its respective plot before understanding its essence – this is key when designing its extension.

Tel Aviv has to respond to the needs of modern-day metropolitan Israel, which has the fastest growing population in the OECD. While there are numerous problems with the new urban master plan, it does provide carefully calibrated answers to the pressures and necessities of today's world.

Having existed for only seventy-one years, Israel is a relatively young country, yet it is still fighting for its very survival. To many, preserving its heritage, especially that of modernism (which not everyone necessarily finds appealing aesthetically), seems like a luxury, especially in light of the existential threats facing the state.

Nonetheless, the conservation plan upholds Geddes' unique ideas and the proportions of the modern city, while allowing for renewal and new development. The heart of the city does not have the privilege of becoming a museum of architecture, but has to continue to serve as the living tissue of Israel's most important metropolis, which keeps on growing and adapting to the needs of contemporary society.

SHIRA LEVY BENYEMINI
THE LIEBLING HOUSE BECOMES THE WHITE CITY CENTER

FOUNDATION OF THE WHITE CITY CENTER

The relationship between culture and the conservation of modernist architectural heritage – especially when viewed in the urban context – is by no means a trivial enterprise; therefore, it took time for the establishment to recognise the need to connect the two through a cultural centre that tells the story of this specific aspect of heritage.

Together with the German government, it was decided to establish a centre that would focus on modern architecture from within a typical building: the Liebling House. As we began working, we decided to follow a more organic process; something that evolves from the needs of the city and the surrounding area to dictate the direction of the future programme. We wanted to cultivate the salient connection between heritage, modernist ideas and values, and the urban culture of the city.

The Liebling House at night, White City Center Tel Aviv, Photo: Yael Schmidt

The Interior during the Renovation, White City Center Tel Aviv, Photo: Yael Schmidt

(bottom left) **Studying old techniques:** Terrazzo workshop, White City Center Tel Aviv, Photo: Yael Schmidt

(bottom right) **Pigments for the walls,** White City Center Tel Aviv, Photo: Yael Schmidt

STEP 1: RETHINKING MODERN ARCHITECTURE CONSERVATION

Until recently, conservation projects focused on physical aspects, for example, how to add more storeys to an existing building. Tel Aviv became an expert on the development of listed historical buildings, yet was occupied by engineering challenges to such an extent that sometimes the spirit of the place and the history of its residents vanished completely. We were looking for ways to engage the community in the idea of conservation.

Since the Liebling House was vacant during the planning process, we were able to develop a unique project: a residency programme titled "The Liebling Project". The project – a collaboration with the Conservation Department of the Tel Aviv-Yafo Municipality – studied the objectives of urban conservation and the future activities of The White City Center. The multidisciplinary team included thirteen artists and scholars exploring urban conservation while developing content for the centre and its conservation process. This ongoing project allowed us to convert the

Liebling House, gradually and naturally, from an introverted residential and office building into a welcoming public space venue. The collaboration between artists and professionals enabled both groups to explore conservation and architecture from different perspectives, inspiring a broad, critical and productive dialogue about the conservation of a modernist building.

The premise of the Liebling Project is that urban-architectural conservation can be more sustainable by studying its implementation in different disciplines and cultural fields. The process and its conclusions helped the professional team promote an holistic conservation strategy that enters into a dialogue with the community and preserves the spirit of the ever-evolving city.

Visitors in the staircase during the Open for renovation project, White City Center Tel Aviv, Photo: Yael Schmidt

Open for renovation, White City Center Tel Aviv, Photo: Yael Schmidt

STEP 2: A TEST CASE OF RETHINKING CONSERVATION: THE OPEN FOR RENOVATION PROJECT

A broader perspective on conservation and an attempt to explore alternatives of intangible conservation have led us to initiate an open renovation that transformed the Liebling House into an experimental lab for different processes while inviting the public to participate and discover the values of these buildings.During the "Open for Renovation" project, we invited the public to visit the Liebling House in a series of lectures, tours, and exhibitions that offered a new perspective. The Liebling House became a live performance, a showcase, and a lab, exposing its layers, its conservation process, and traditional crafts while promoting a better understanding of the qualities of modernist architecture.

THE WHITE CITY CENTER AT THE LIEBLING HOUSE

The WCC will operate at the Max Liebling House (1936), one of the listed buildings around Bialik Square, once the beating heart of Tel Aviv. Commissioned by Tony and Max Liebling, acclaimed architect Dov Karmi designed a distinctive international style building that stands as an antithesis of its neighbor - the eclectic, decorated home of national poet Haim Nahman Bialik.

The Center seeks to explore and highlight the unique modernist architectural and urban World Heritage Site of Tel Aviv's White City and aspires for excellence in the fields of research and professional training and conservation. These objectives will be achieved by establishing a leading hub for professionals, residents, visitors, and the public engaged in conservation and urban development, with an emphasis on modern architecture. The Center will study the physical, theoretical, cultural, and social aspects of conservation and engage the public through a range of activities, serving as a platform for urbanism and architectural appreciation among professionals, as well as residents of all ages.

By consolidating all these functions, the Center will reinforce the bilateral relationship between Germany and Israel through joint projects.

The Center is scheduled to open in September 2019, the centennial of the Bauhaus school.

(right page) **Interiors and Details of the Liebling House,**
Photos: Yael Schmidt

The Liebling House becomes the White City Center

SHMUEL GROAG
THE TEL AVIV-JAFFA WORKSHOP

The workshop in Tel Aviv-Jaffa, focused on two houses in Tel-Aviv and Jaffa respectively, both designed by less well-known Bauhaus graduates, the architects Shmuel Mistechkin and Chanan Frenkel. Neither of the two chosen sites – the Mestechkin Kiryati House on the corner of Rothschild Boulevard and Habima Square (No. 4 Habima Square) and Frenkel's "blood bank" building in Jaffa (Shivtey Yisrael 48) – are listed and do not form part of the Israeli Bauhaus legacy. As such, part of the importance of the workshop and the exhibition is to help in the process of averting the threat of impending destruction.

The workshop was based on a series of lectures and tours by leading architects in the field of the International Style movement in Israel: Sharon Golan Yaron, Director of Programmes at the White City Center, Tel Aviv, Prof. Zvi Efrat and Prof. Yuval Yaski, Shira Sprecher, Bezalel Academy of Arts and Design, Jersualem, Jeremie Hoffmann, Head of the Conservation Department, Municipality of Tel Aviv, Micha Levin, architectural historian, Shenkar-Ramat Gan, Lilach Harel, Groag-Harel architects, Tel Aviv and Yehudith

Kiryati, Israel Development & Building Co. Ltd. On the one hand, the main idea was to raise the awareness of the work of Mestechkin and Frenkel and on the other, to simulate the issues and problems arising from additions to heritage sites in Tel Aviv. Because of the pressure on real estate in Israel in general and in Tel Aviv-Jaffa in particular, many of the buildings, even if they are listed, are experiencing massive change in the form of large additions or extensions. The existing town plan and development scheme (2650B), which forms part of the management plan for Tel Aviv's "White City" World Heritage Site, allows for an addition of up to six storeys to buildings, even though the majority of them were designed with just three floors.

WORKSHOP PROGRAM

The first day of the workshop was dedicated to site analysis through different media in order to understand the significance of the buildings. Each small mixed group of students had to prepare a general abstract impression of the site using different media including sketches,

(top) **Sharon Golan Yaron presenting the Liebling House to the students**, Photo: Eléna Hinsch

(bottom) **Micha Levin, Shmuel Groag and Katrin Kessler**, Photo: Eléna Hinsch

Sketching first impressions
on Habima Square,
Photo: Eléna Hinsch

music, film, et cetera. The groups were given guidance in how to analyse the site, each of them with a different focus, but all of them had to draw some typical details of the building in order to understand the aesthetics and materials of the period.

The directive for the first two days was to present:

- location: present the site in its location by drawing it in different scales, including indoor and outdoor. Archive work on the neighbourhood; historical analysis

- details: measure and draw, freehand and later on the computer, typical details of the original building. Archive work building details
- photographs and interviews: photograph and analyse the building in its surroundings, facades, details, people, action, analogies from other buildings , et cetera. Archive work on analogies and the spirit of the era in which the building was created
- landscape: garden and vegetation: original plans ,fences, elements, trees, analogies from other gardens. Archive work on landscape planning of the period

- historic changes: analyse typical elements of the International Style using a 3D-model, timeline of additions and extensions. Archive work on elements and materials
- statutory town planning documents and biographies: analyse the existing building through comparison of historical town plan schemes and building permits.

Colour samples in the Liebling House –
dry pigments on the floor, painted on the wall,
Photo: Éléna Hinsch

Working in the workshop on Bialik Square,
Photo: Éléna Hinsch

Klaus Tragbar, Regina Stephan and Ulrich Knufinke in front of
the Bezalel Academy in Jerusalem, Photo: Éléna Hinsch

The second part of the workshop focused on proposed interventions and building additions based on the specific significance identified by the students and on the brief site analysis. The students were given some theoretical background and examples from around the world in the form of two lectures delivered by the teachers, focusing on different ethics and practices at work when adding to or extending heritage sites. As a result of the experience in Dessau-Törten, most of the students had already acquired relevant skills for the task in hand and were able to present plans, sections and virtual 3D-models after two days of intensive work.

Critical to the results of the workshop were two important facts, namely that Chanan Frenkel's blood bank was built in the middle of a Palestinian neighbourhood in 1950's Jaffa, i.e. in a highly contested area, and that it is currently being used as a temporary site for a democratic school. The two different extremes, we chose for the workshop one in the heart of the White City and the other in the heart of the gentrification process in Jaffa, exposed the students to the complex issues arising from conservation in Tel-Aviv-Jaffa today.

KATRIN KESSLER AND VLADIMIR LEVIN
THE KIRYATI HOUSE AND ITS ARCHITECT SHMUEL MESTECHKIN

Although Tel Aviv is renowned for its Bauhaus structures, in reality there are only a few buildings in the White City that were actually designed by architects trained at the Bauhaus in Germany. The Kiryati House on Kikar Habima, designed and built by Shmuel Mestechkin between 1938 and 1940, is one of them.

Shmuel Mestechkin was born in 1908 in Vasylkiv, Russia (now Ukraine), about 30 km southwest of Kiev. As his father had died during Shmuel's childhood, his older brother, Mordechai became head of the family. (1) As a committed Zionist and member of the youth association Zeirei Zion, he immigrated to Palestine in 1921 in response to the pogroms against Jews instigated in 1919, which also affected his hometown. He changed his name to Kiryati ("small town" in Hebrew, like "Mestechkin" in Ukrainian). Fifteen-year-old Shmuel, his mother and three sisters followed Mordechai in 1923 and settled in Tel Aviv. They would continue to be a closely-knit family in the years that followed.

Shmuel became a founding member of the socialist youth movement Histadrut No'ar Ha-oved ve-Ha-lomed (Federation of Young

Shmuel Mistechkin,
Kiryati House, Tel Aviv,
1938–1940

Students and Workers) in 1924. In 1928, he erected a tower for the youth movement's summer camp on the Carmel mountain range, which would prompt him to study architecture. His friend Shlomo Gur later integrated the tower into his homa u-migdal concept (wall and stockade) as a security measure in fifty-seven kibbutzim. (2) Since Mestechkin didn't have the qualifications to study architecture at the Technion in Haifa, he applied for a place at the Bauhaus in Dessau. He was accepted and began his studies on 4 October 1931; he was taught by Josef Albers and Wassily Kandinsky, among others. The community and ways of working at the Bauhaus reminded him of the appreciation of craftsmanship, the spirit and socialist mentality he had encountered in Noar Ha-oved.

As a result of the rise to power of the Nazis in 1933 and/or the subsequent dissolution of the Bauhaus on 20 July of the same year, Mestechkin seems to have travelled to Vienna to study art, whence he returned to Palestine in 1934 by the latest.

He initially found employment with Josef Neufeld (1899-1980), who also hailed from the area of modern-day Ukraine. He also collaborated closely with his brother Mordechai, who worked as a surveyor, engineer and town planner for the Keren Kayemet (the Jewish National Fund whose primary focus was on land acquisition up until 1948). In contrast to his brother, Shmuel remained true to his socialist ethos professionally as well: instead of working in the private sector, he devoted himself exclusively to the design of public works, (3)

for example the Noar Ha-oved centres in Tel Aviv and Haifa, as well as a sports stadium and other buildings on the Givat Ram campus of the Hebrew University of Jerusalem, among many other public works. However, he was known best for being the architect of kibbutzim. As a freelance architect, by 1937 he had already built numerous communal facilities in the Na'an, Ashdot Yacov and Ramat Hakovesh kibbutzim. He worked for the Hagana (4) between 1937 and

View from the apartment on the third floor towards Habima Square, Photo: Ulrich Knufinke, 2019

1939 on the construction of fortified kibbutzim in keeping with the homa u-migdal principle and was senior architect of the technical department of the Ha-Kibbutz Ha-artzi movement from 1943 to 1973. (5) He designed various building projects for about sixty kibbutzim in this capacity: residential buildings, children's houses, dining rooms, schools and farm buildings. As a widely acclaimed Israeli architect, he served as President of the Israeli Association of Engineers, Architects and Graduates in Technological Sciences from 1959 to 1963 and was honoured for his work in 1980.

However, Mestechkin did make one exception to his principle of eschewing private-sector commissions: he designed several private residential buildings in Tel Aviv for his brother Mordechai, including two apartment blocks. (6) The two so-called Kiryati Houses were built at 12-14 Rupin Street and 4 Kikar Ha-bima, opposite Oskar Kaufmann's Habima Theatre, which has been under construction since 1933. The siblings and their mother moved into the property at 4 Kikar Ha-bima. Although Shmuel subsequently left to start his own family after his wedding, he returned after his divorce. He died there on 2 June 2004. (7)

The four-storey apartment block on the corner of Kikar Ha-Bima / Rothschild Boulevard consists of two sections of buildings at different, staggered

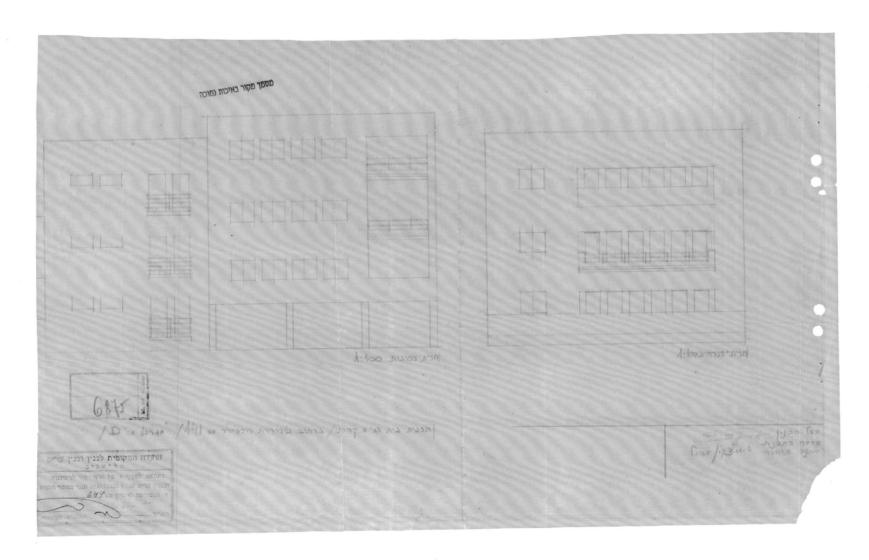

מסמך מקור באיכות נמוכה

חזית צפונית 00:1/

חזית דרומית 00:1/

82   Katrin Kessler and Vladimir Levin

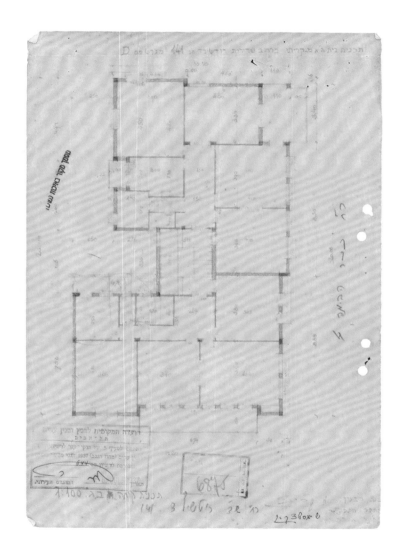

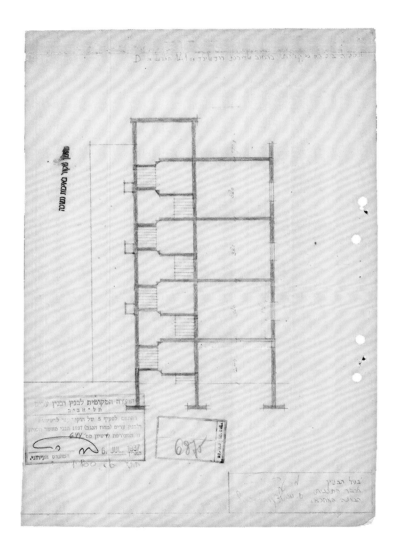

heights connected by a central staircase. Its proportions and façade closely resemble those of the Ha-noar Ha-oved building in Tel Aviv, (8) which Mestechkin also built in the late-1930s . The levels of the two parts of the building are staggered by half a storey, forming a split-level configuration; the ground floor is open generously on both sides of the street and was obviously used as business premises. Each of the spacious apartments on the floors above have four rooms as well as adjoining rooms and at least one balcony. Some of the windows are still fitted with the original extendable blinds that afford protection from the sun and allow the rooms to be ventilated.

The three-storey building overlooking Rothschild Boulevard has cantilevered balconies on the upper two storeys projecting from the façade, the smaller ones of which bearing a strong resemblance to the Prellerhaus balconies at the Bauhaus in Dessau. By contrast, the balconies of the four-storey section of the building at the back sit in a recessed niche, which runs from top to bottom of the building, lending depth to the structure and forming an exciting contrast with the adjacent punched window façade. Passersby are unlikely to notice these details as they surge past this corner building today in a seemingly never-ending flow of traffic. However, it is worthwhile taking a closer look at the building, as a second glance reveals quite a number of period features. Although the entrance area and stairwell were redesigned in the 1990s, the railing with its interesting solution for the handrail in the corners is original. The fact that an apartment replete with its original fittings still exists today is something of a minor miracle.

Paradoxically, today's residents, some of whom are descendants of the Mestechkin family, do not seem to share the Shmuel Mestechkin's sentiments, who told the founder of the Bauhaus Center in Tel Aviv, Michael Gross in an interview that " ... one should not cling on to the old nostalgically, but instead demolish all Bauhaus-style buildings in Tel Aviv and replace them with new structures, because this would be more consistent with the modernist philosophy of the Bauhaus, according to which the new is more useful to people than the old, simply because it is more functional and more suited to their needs." (9)

Happily, the Kiryati-Mestechkin family takes a different view, which has resulted in the preservation of this beautiful Bauhaus-inspired building, which, one hopes, will be saved for posterity.

Annotations

(1) Muki Tsur and Yuval Danieli, eds. Livnot u-lehibanot ba - Sefer Shmuel Mistechkin. Adrichalut ha-Kibutz be-Israel (Tel Aviv 2008), p. 15. ("To build and to be built in the Land: Shmuel Mestechkin Book. Architecture in the Kibbutz".)

(2) Tsur and Danieli, Livnot u-lehibanot ba, p. 25.

(3) Lydia Aisenberg, "Designing for the Collective: Shmuel Mestechkin", Jerusalem Post (24 December 24, 2008). https://www.jpost.com/Local-Israel/Around-Israel/Designing-for-the-collective-Shmuel-Mestechkin. Last accessed 24.5.19.

(4) Tsur and Danieli, Livnot u-lehibanot ba, p. 12. The Hagana was a Zionist paramilitary organisation in Palestine during the British Mandate (1920-1948).Shmuel Burmil and Ruth Enis, The Changing Landscape of Utopia: The Landscape and Gardens of the Kibbutz (Worms,2012), p. 189. Ha-Kibbutz ha-Artzi was the umbrella organisation of the kibbutz movement.

(5) Tsur and Danieli, Livnot u-lehibanot ba, p. 17.

(6) Mestechkin left a private archive, which is kept at the Yad Ya'ari Research and Documentation Centre.

(7) Cf. Tsur and Danieli, Livnot u-lehibanot ba, p. 22. Although there is a photograph, no address is given.

(8) Cf. Chaimowicz, "Der Schatz von Tel Aviv", ZEITmagazin.

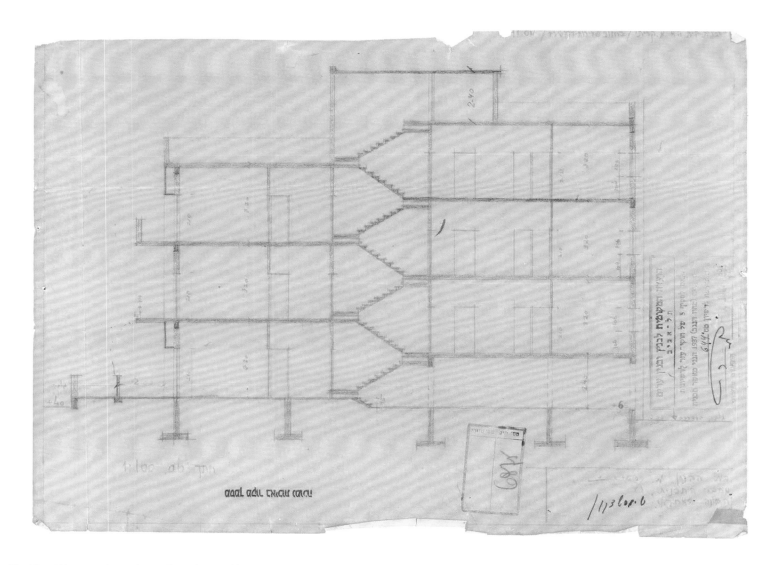

ULRICH KNUFINKE

MODERNITY IN A TIME CAPSULE
An apartment in the Kiryati House in Tel Aviv

A friendly conversation with the niece of the architect Mestechkin, an arrangement to meet on the penultimate day of the trip – an event that opens up a door into the life and living in Tel Aviv eighty years ago. When Shmuel Mestechkin built a block of flats on the corner of Rothschild Boulevard and Kikar Habima for his large family in 1938, it kick-started the development of this district of Tel Aviv. Today, with the Rubina Auditorium and the Habima Theatre in its orbit, this area is one of the urban and cultural centres not only of the city, but of Israel as a whole. The architect and several family members moved into the four-storey, cuboid corner house, the view of which is now largely blocked by trees. Some of his descendants live here today.

As one might expect, a lot has changed in eight decades in and around the block of flats. All the more surprising is a corner flat on the third floor: uninhabited for several years, many of the original fittings are still preserved here, which elsewhere fell prey to renovation and refurbishment long ago – a veritable time capsule of extraordinary significance.

The front door leads into a small hall with a cupboard as a built-in wardrobe. A small room to the left was added to another apartment. The large living room is situated in the prominent corner block in Habima Square replete with a long east-facing balcony and a small exit to the north. An internal hallway with a suspended ceiling to provide storage space leads from the entrance hall toward the south: it connects with the bedroom on the left, i.e. to the east toward Rothschild Boulevard, and the WC and the bathroom to the right, facing west, and at the end of the hallway the kitchen with a small West-facing balcony. The floors are tiled, as is common in Tel Aviv. Many of the fittings, such as doors, light switches and power sockets, have been preserved in their original condition. The walls and ceilings have been redecorated several times over the years – whether they were originally painted white or a light grey-blue is currently largely unrecognisable.

The wooden windows with blinds probably date from the 1930s; although a bit stiff, they are still in working order. In the era before the advent of air conditioning, shade and ventilation were at a premium when living in the hot and humid conditions in Tel Aviv. The White City architects responded to these climatic conditions and adapted their modern architecture accordingly: generous use of glazing, typical for Central Europe, was completely inappropriate here; natural ventilation and shade took priority. Mestechkin made sure that transverse ventilation was possible in all rooms in the flats, for example, he specifically installed a ventilation opening between the bedroom and kitchen, and above the door there is a flap to the stairwell, which also facilitates transverse ventilation.

The bathroom (with the original bathtub, shower, taps and tiles), the WC (with all original fittings) and the kitchen have been preserved in almost pristine condition. Based on the model of the "Frankfurt Kitchen", all salient kitchen functions have been fitted into a small space so that the stove, sink, worktop, floor and wall cabinets, as well as a pantry ventilated from the balcony are within easy reach. The fitted furniture clearly designed specifically for this room bears witness to the modern, functional aspirational aspect of living in Tel Aviv, which – despite the other-

Modernity in a time capsule

wise well-appointed tenor of the residence – is apparently to be achieved without the aid of a housekeeper.

Unfortunately, the original furniture from the flat that was not fitted has been lost; there is a wardrobe in the bedroom, which did not belong to the original fittings and must have been installed at a later date, and also possibly the

ceiling light in this room is a relic from the 1930s.

It is likely that most of the period structural elements will be removed in the event of future renovation. Therefore, a thorough documentation of the apartment block's current physical condition containing a detailed survey of site measurements would be of prodigious importance for our understanding of and knowledge about everyday

life and living in the White City during the 1930s. The floor plan design and the block's fittings illustrate that the architect Mestechkin, who rose to prominence as a designer of kibbutzim, systematically pursued a functional approach in the design of a house that one might have called "middle class", which he then implemented in the most sophisticated detail. An historical

Kiryati-House, Tel Aviv, Apartment on third floor,
Photos: Ulrich Knufinke, 2019

study could also clarify who the residents of this flat and the entire block actually were; indeed, perhaps it is also possible to glean even more information about the furnishings and life in these rooms via private photos or personal memories of the inhabitants.

Be that as it may, the preservation of such an object poses an enormous challenge: it is debateable whether individual fittings – e.g. the bathroom, WC and kitchen – can or should be removed and transferred to a museum context. However, preserving this remarkable time capsule of modernity *in situ* and granting the public access to it under the provision of dutiful care would be the ideal solution for such an unusual and remarkable space.

SAMADAR AUKAL

CHANAN FRENKEL AND THE BLOOD BANK IN JAFFA

Chanan Frenkel was born as Hans-Hermann Frenkel on 22 July 1905 to a Jewish family in Halle, Germany. (1) His father was a merchant and industrialist. Frenkel graduated from the Reform Realgymnasium (grammar school) in his hometown in 1921 and continued his education after two failed apprenticeships in the Netherlands where he focused on farming. His study was tailored to the same end as his membership of the Hechalutz youth movement where he trained to become a shepherd and related work, namely migration to Palestine. Since his youth, Frenkel had been passionate about the concept of Zionism and had already become a member of the Kempde Jewish Society in 1920. In 1926, he helped build the Cheruth Kibbutz in Hamelin, the first Kibbutz in Germany. In 1928 at the age of twenty-three, he moved to Palestine and joined the Ein Harod Kibbutz in Emek-Jisrael and Givat Brenner northwest of Jerusalem, which was founded in the same year.

Hans-Hermann (Chanan) Frenkel, Blood Bank, Jaffa, 1953–1956

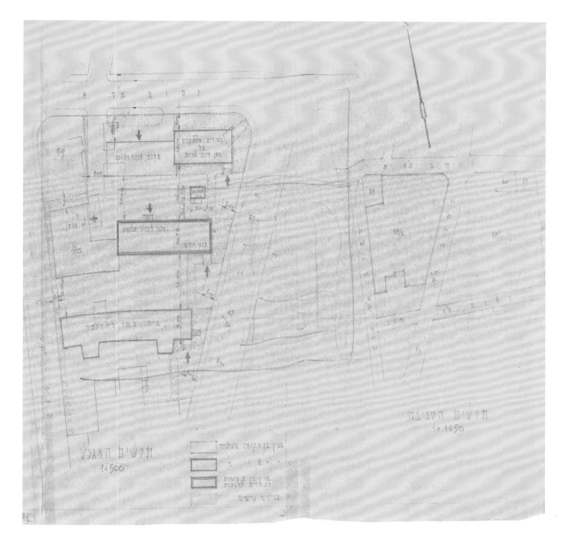

In 1929 Frenkel moved to Dessau in Germany to study architecture and design at the Bauhaus. At this time the bau-ausbau (build / extend) building department was under the direction of Ludwig Mies van der Rohe and Ludwig Hilberseimer. Frenkel graduated on 15 August 1932, receiving Bauhaus Diploma No. 91.

Alongside Frenkel, there were other students at the Bauhaus who shared his enthusiasm for Zionism, such as Ricarda Meltzer, Heinz Schwerin and Munio Weinraub who eventually relocated to Palestine. Despite not being Jewish, Meltzer and Schwerin, as communists, shared the dream of a better future. The three used the skills they acquired at the Bauhaus as tools to express their political opinions through architecture and photography, among other things.

Following his graduation from the Bauhaus, Frenkel returned to Palestine and settled in Tel Aviv, where he was more than eager to participate as an architect in the construction of the new state. He worked in several architectural offices, including the firms of Carl Rubin, Elsa Gidoni and Eliezer Zeisler. From the latter part of 1936 on, the young architect worked in the

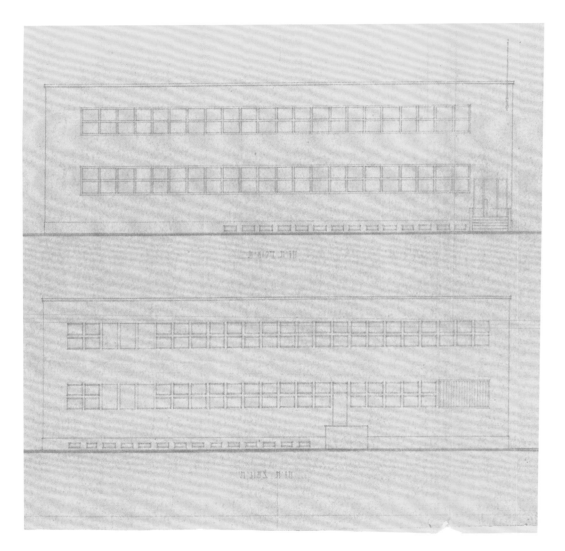

Levant Fair studios in Tel Aviv, while helping with
the preparations for the Palestinian pavilions at
the World Exhibition in Paris 1937 and New York,
1939/40.

During the same period, he planned a house
for the Eulau Family in Khedira in 1938, a design
that was subsequently published in the contemporary architectural press. From 1940 onward,
he worked in the Public Works Department of
the British Mandatory Agency and, as a British
soldier, he took part in the excavations in
Niniveh, Iraq.

In 1945, just three years before the establishment of Israel, Frenkel took part in the "Contributions to Planning in Palestine: Kahane – Frenkel
– Trostler – Witt" exhibition at the Bezalel Jewish
National Museum in Jerusalem. In 1948, he
came first in a competition for the design of a
bus station in Netanya; however, the project was
never realised. During the 1950s Frenkel specia-
lised in constructing hospitals, designing his most
recognised work in 1953: the blood bank in Jaffa
for Magen David Adom, a Jewish aid agency.
Founded in 1930 in Tel Aviv, it is a sister organisation of the Red Cross.

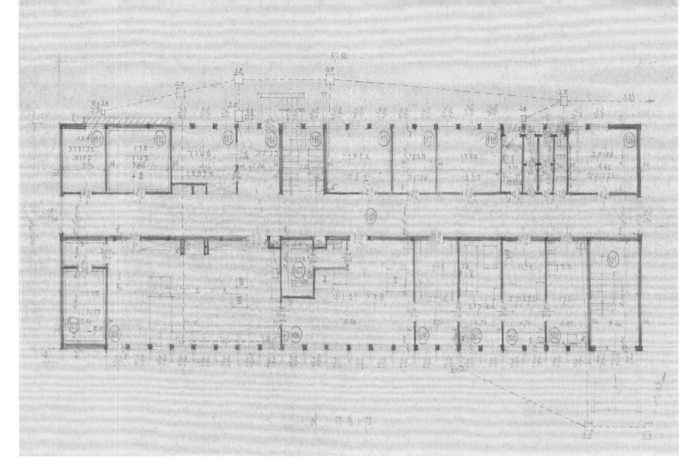

Magen David Adom (MDA) built the first blood banks in Tel Aviv, Jerusalem and Haifa from 1947 onward. The Israeli government provided the site for the building in Jaffa which was constructed between 1953 and 1965. Chanan Frenkel, who at that time was the head of the Keren Nechut Construction Department of the Kupat Cholim Union Health Insurance Fund, was commissioned to plan the Blood Fractionation and Plasma Dying (Research) Institute.

His plan envisaged a two-storey building, the main southerly aspect of which features horizontal ribbon windows. The sun shades extending far in front of the windows is another striking feature, which underline the building's character as a storage facility and also provide protective shade for the windows. The main entrance is also situated on this side of the

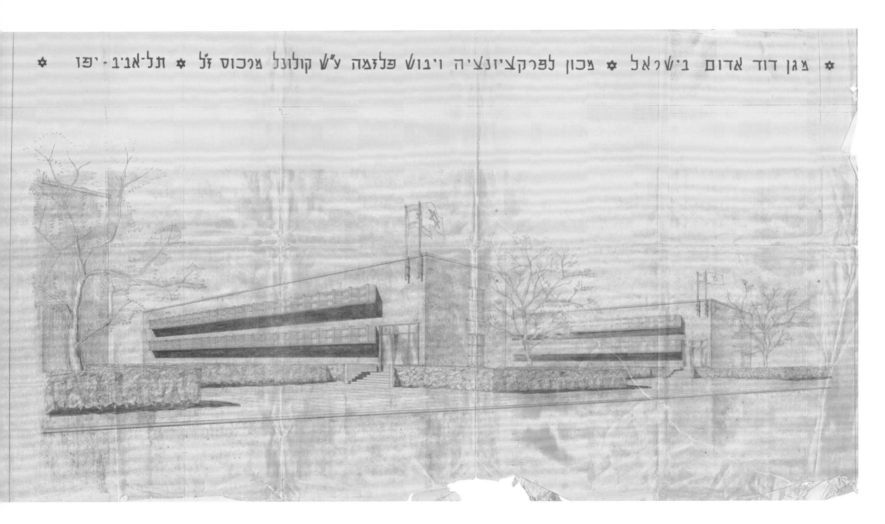

מגן דוד אדום בישראל ✡ מכון לפרקציונציה ויבוש פלזמה ע״ש קולונל מרכוס ז״ל ✡ תל־אביב ־ יפו ✡

Perspective with a second never realised building, City Engineer Archive, Municipality of Tel Aviv-Yafo

building from Dr. Erlich St. (historically known as Street Number 8), which is enhanced by two flagpoles attached to the façade, which project high above the building. The side and the rear façades are much simpler in design. The building is boxlike, angular and has a flat roof. Frenkel's studies at the Bauhaus certainly influenced the design of the building, as well as his personal interpretation of the State of Israel and the International Style, which dominated the city of Tel Aviv. The fact that the foundation stone was laid by Vera Weizmann, the wife of the first President of Israel, Chaim Weizmann, bears witness to the significance this building had for the fledgling Jewish State.

Frenkel died in Tel Aviv in 1957 aged fifty-one, a mere twelve months after the successful completion of the blood bank. Even though not many of Frenkel's designs were implemented in Israel, his vision is dominant in the project and it is also possible to trace Frenkel's sources of inspiration in his work and the things that influenced his design choices.

The building was extended at a later date: the second building was erected at right angles to

the first on the western side of the site. The third building was located on the southern side of the site and served as an instructional facility. The buildings had their own individual entrances from Shivtei Israel St. (historically known as Street Number 7).

At present, the blood bank building functions as the "Kehila Democratic School". The group of buildings, including the original blood bank, are still in their original form, however, they are poorly maintained and there have also been various other additions to the buildings over the years.

Annotations

(1) Myra Warhaftig, Sie legten den Grundstein, Leben und Wirken deutschsprachiger jüdischer Architekten in Palästina 1918-1948 (Tübingen and Berlin, 1996), p. 144f. Illustr. cf. p. 145 bottom of the page: letterhead of the family firm S. Frenkel in Halle / Saale.

(2) On Frenkel, cf. in particular: Ines Sonder, Werner Möller, Ruwen Egri, Vom Bauhaus nach Palästina. Chanan Frenkel, Ricarda und Heinz Schwerin (Leipzig, 2013). Edition: Bauhaus Taschenbuch 6.

KLAUS TRAGBAR

ADDITIONS TO BUILDINGS IN EUROPE – A FEW OF THEM AT LEAST

The history of every piece of architecture commences with the design of the building, the architect's overall creative concept and artistic vision, the intention of the client, the technical and constructional possibilities and the prevalent artistic currents of the time. However, the completion of a building by no means signals the end of the story; on the contrary, the existing, often barely finished structure is often converted, rebuilt or extended, be it for an adapted or a wholly new purpose. This is true of the Colosseum in Rome whose three-storey façade of arched arcades was augmented by a fourth, admittedly largely closed storey just before its completion in 79 CE, while retaining the structure of the façade, and likewise of the Palazzo Medici-Riccardi in Florence, which, using exactly the same architectural language as the original structure built between 1446 and 1451, was enlarged from 1670 onward by seven axes.

Two of the most common variants of further construction are named in the preceding paragraph (1): copying existing stock exactly in favour of a uniform appearance in order to bury traces of the building's history in the homogeneity of the whole structure, as is the case with the Palazzo Medici-Riccardi; leaning toward characteristic motifs of the existing building, which are not copied, but interpreted and varied in such a way that they both connect to the building yet at the same time also highlight the addition. The third essential variant is further construction aimed at contrast, through which the new additions to the existing building – by virtue of their decidedly independent architectural language – enter into a dialogue with it.

Contemporary examples of the first variant, the exact copy, have become extremely rare in times in which architecture is perceived to be a hyperindividualised profession. Examples of the second variant are the reconstruction of Franzensfeste fortress north of Brixen / Bressanone by Markus Scherer and Walter Dietl (2005–2009) and the reconstruction by David Chipperfield Architects (1998–2009) of the Neues Museum in Berlin, which was partially demolished during the Second World War (3). Both buildings evince a careful approach: the sensitive adoption of existing proportions and individual architectural features, such as openings and structural elements and their interpretation in terms of a contemporary architectural language. Examples of a stylistic dialogue between the new and the old abound in the works of Carlo Scarpa, viz. the Museo di Castelvecchio in Verona (1958–1964, 1968/69, 1973) (4) and the Fondazione Querini Stampalia in Venice (1961–1963) to name but two (5), as well in

Franzensfeste Brixen/Bressanone,
New Entrance by Scherer + Dietl 2005-09

Friedrich August Stüler,
Neues Museum Berlin,
1843–55,
Reconstruction by
David Chipperfield
1998–2009

Karljosef Schattner's oeuvre, for example in the careful rebuilding of the Ulmer Hof (1978–1980) (6) and the orphanage (1985–1988) (7) for the Catholic University of Eichstätt. Both architects have mastered the art of reconciling autonomy in architectural expression with a sensitive approach to the existing structure.

Annotations

(1) As an introduction here, cf. Oskar Spital-Frenking, Architektur und Denkmal. Der Umgang mit bestehender Bausubstanz. Entwicklungen, Positionen, Projekte (Leinfelden-Echterdingen, 2000); Christian Schittich, Im Detail. Bauen im Bestand. Umnutzung, Ergänzung, Neuschöpfung (Munich, 2003); Johannes Cramer and Stefan Breitling, Architektur im Bestand. Planung, Entwurf, Ausführung (Basel, Boston and Berlin, 2007).

(2) Cf. Andreas Gottlieb Hempel, "Kampflos übergeben. Festung Franzensfeste bei Brixen", in Baumeister 107.2010, (1), pp. 60-71; Marco Mulazzani, "Markus Scherer, Walter Dietl. Recupero della Franzensfeste, Fortezza, Bolzano" in Casabella 783, 73.2009, pp. 52-61.

(3) Cf. inter alia, Andres Lepik and Friederike von Rauch, eds, Neues Museum (Ostfildern, 2009); Berlin State Museum and others, eds, Das Neue Museum Berlin. Konservieren, Restaurieren, Weiterbauen im Welterbe (Leipzig, 2009). Cf. also the interesting juxtaposition made by Alice Klose in her study Der Wiederaufbau des Neuen Museums in Berlin als Inszenierung der eigenen Geschichte. Der Wandel im Umgang mit Fragmenten im Vergleich zum Wiederaufbau der Glyptothek in München, diss. LMU Munich, 2015, urn: nbn: de: bvb: 19-181981.

(4) Cf. inter alia Francesco Dal Co and Giuseppe Mazzariol, Carlo Scarpa (Milan, 1984), p. 119, 159–163; Carlo Scarpa, Museo di Castelvecchio (Stuttgart and London, 2016).

(5) Cf. inter alia Dal Co and Mazzariol, Carlo Scarpa, p. 124; Francesco Dal Co and Sergio Polano, Fondazione Querini Stampalia (Milan, 2015).

(6) Cf. inter alia Wolfgang Pehnt, Karljosef Schattner. Ein Architekt aus Eichstätt (Stuttgart, 1988), pp. 80-89; Wolfgang Jean Stock, ed., Architektur und Fotografie. Korrespondenzen (Basel, 2002), pp. 96-107. For the first overview of his oeuvre, cf. Ulrich Conrads and Manfred Sack, Karljosef Schattner (Braunschweig and Wiesbaden, 1983).

(7) Cf. inter alia Pehnt, Karljosef Schattner, pp. 142-150; Stock, Architektur und Photografie, pp. 68-73.

(left) **Castelvecchio Verona,**
Entrance 1 by Carlo Scarpa 1954–64

(right) **Karljosef Schattner, Catholic University Eichstätt, Faculty of psychology in the former orphanage, 1985–88**

THE STUDENT´S WORKS
BLOOD BANK, JAFFA

Lena Schwinn, first impression of the former blood bank in Jaffa, 2019

BLOOD BANK – PROJECT 1

Danit Fisch, Nohar Hochberg, Sharon Pery

(from left to right:) **Danit Fisch, Sharon Pery, Nohar Hochberg, Jerusalem**

BLOOD BANK MATERIALS

BLOOD BANK

BLOOD BANK

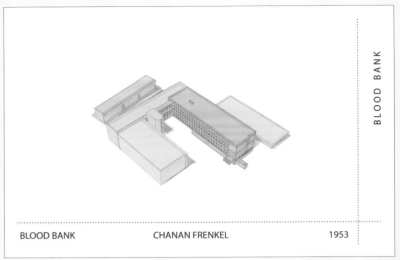

BLOOD BANK

BLOOD BANK CHANAN FRENKEL 1953

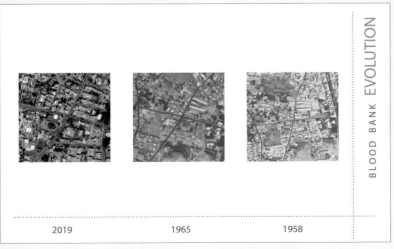

BLOOD BANK EVOLUTION

2019 1965 1958

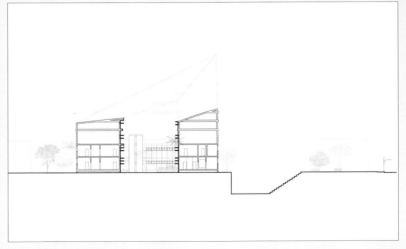

Blood Bank – Project 2: Central Public Space

Marius Druyen, Florian Fuchs, Mor Shapir, Ortal Shecter

The "CPS" design for the blood bank in Jaffa is intended to disinter and spotlight the significance of Frenkel's architecture. Over the years, the historic building has been augmented by a number of extensions that are almost invisibly joined on to the existing structural fabric. In order to accentuate the original quality of the building, the annexes should be demolished to create space for new architecture.

As accommodation is very scarce in Tel Aviv, provision for student lodgings is to be made in the upper storeys of the large L-shaped building. The ground floor will be used as a public library.

In the blood bank itself, a communal working area is intended to revive this historic building and transform it into a public space. This can be utilised for any number of leisure activities in order to revitalise the building and integrate it into the everyday life of its residents. This concept not only involves a fundamental reactivation of the building through special architectural interventions, but also by promoting the importance of the place for the residents.

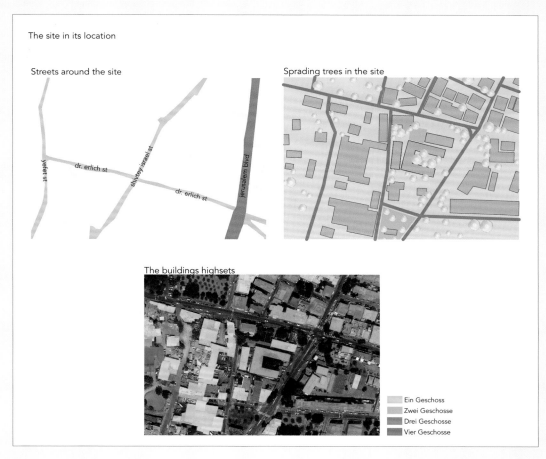

The site in its location

Streets around the site

Sprading trees in the site

The buildings highsets

Ein Geschoss
Zwei Geschosse
Drei Geschosse
Vier Geschosse

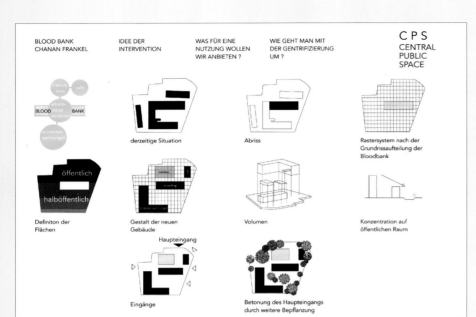

BLOOD BANK
CHANAN FRANKEL

IDEE DER
INTERVENTION

WAS FÜR EINE
NUTZUNG WOLLEN
WIR ANBIETEN ?

WIE GEHT MAN MIT
DER GENTRIFIZIERUNG
UM ?

CPS
CENTRAL
PUBLIC
SPACE

öffentlich

halböffentlich

Definiton der
Flächen

derzeitige Situation

Abriss

Rastersystem nach der
Grundrissaufteilung der
Bloodbank

Gestalt der neuen
Gebäude

Volumen

Konzentration auf
öffentlichen Raum

Haupteingang

Eingänge

Betonung des Haupteingangs
durch weitere Bepflanzung

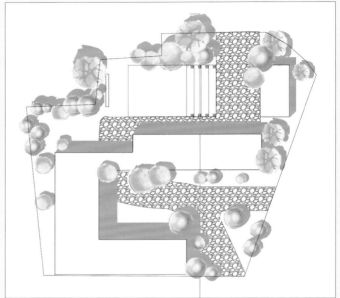

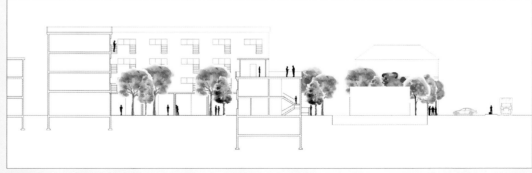

(from left to right:) **Ortal Shecter and Mor Shapir, Jerusalem, Marius Druyen and Florian Fuchs, Mainz, Photo: Éléna Hinsch**

Blood Bank, Jaffa

Blood Bank – Project 3: The Green Gate – Analysis

Inna Berenfeld, Paulina Knodel, Adam Tal

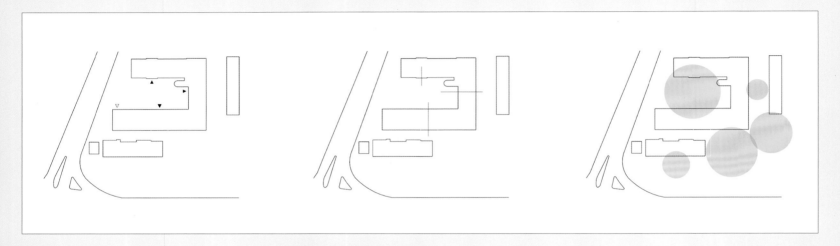

ACCESS

Access through the main entrance leading directly into the courtyard. A further three entrances to the building are located here. Although the original entrance is permanently locked, it is in very good condition. The flow of movement in and out of the building creates a sense of fluid transition which the children make use of equally for their games and work activities.

SCHOOL PLAYGROUNDS

The main school playground is located at the heart of the building. The atmosphere is pleasant and the profusion of trees affords welcome shade. The other areas are arranged outside the U-shaped building, creating a more detached air.

Blood Bank – Project 3: The Green Gate – Design Proposal

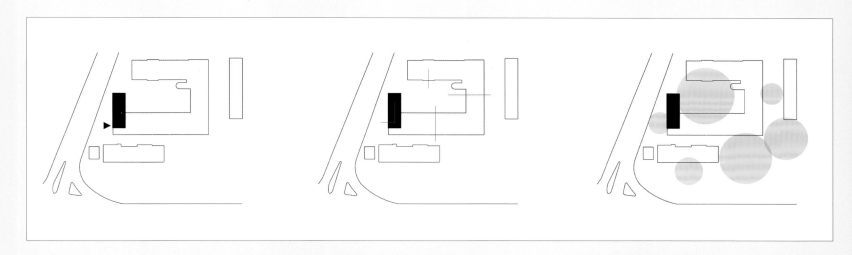

ACCESS

Access through a new entrance: a glass block that slides into the existing building. This creates a visual relationship between internal and external space; however, to enter the school proper one has to pass through security.

FLOW THROUGH THE BUILDING

The current status will be retained – with the proviso that after entering the building, an unauthorised person will now no longer find him/herself in the courtyard.

SCHOOL PLAYGROUNDS

The existing areas are to be retained. The square in front of the school will be enhanced and rendered more inviting by the new building.

Blood Bank – Project 3: The Green Gate – Design Proposal

gardening

entrance
+ security

DESIGN PROPOSAL – FINAL VERSION
(simplifying the idea from the workshop)

The presence of the two palm trees perpetuates the motif of a natural green gate. The idea of the design is to reinforce this motif by placing the new entrance at this point. Glass was chosen in order to set the new building off optically. Its inherent transparency and lightness provide a contrast to the weighty mass of the blood bank building.

The glass block slides into the existing fabric of the building. It encloses the entrance stairs so that they can be used once more. Having entered the building, one can either access the courtyard via the stairs or proceed directly to the hallway. To ensure ongoing security for the school, a fence is still required. As a result, the support grid for

the glass structure also continues on the outside. Instead of glass, however, there is a fence made of shrubs. Upkeep of this fence will also be a part of the pupils' gardening activity as the garden beds are situated immediately behind it.

(from left to right:) Inna Berenfeld, Jerusalem,
Paulina Knodel, Mainz, Adam Tal, Jerusalem,
Photo: Eléna Hinsch

Blood Bank – Project 4: Confetti

Sophie Gumpold, Nirav Patel

The structured plaster façade is a medium, which the residents and users can harness creatively. Thus, Frenkel's building is revisited in its original form and the school gains more space for its pupils.

The historical section of the blood bank is at the heart of the design, as well as its current use as a site for children. New pavilions serve as places of learning, harmonising with the concept of the Democratic School and form small courtyards as places of development for the pupils.

Nirav Patel, Jerusalem, Sophie Gumpold, Innsbruck,
Photo: Eléna Hinsch

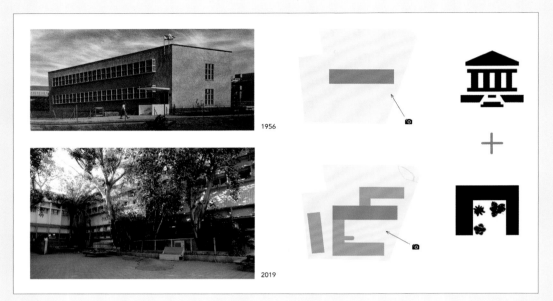

1956

2019

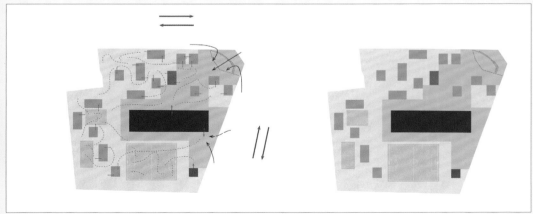

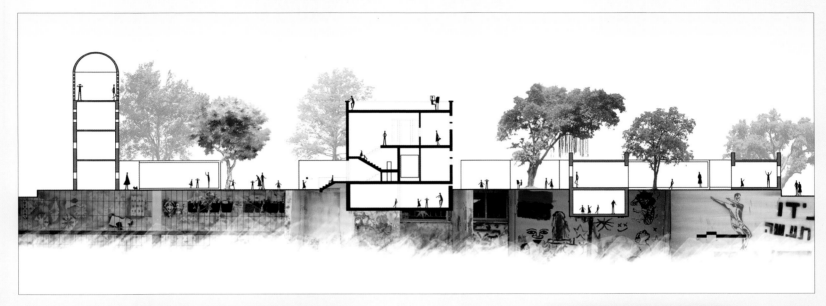

BLOOD BANK – PROJECT 5

Keren Frizigon, Shai Litvak, Lena Schwinn

IDEA

The building is currently being used by the Kehila Democratic School. This use should continue. The blood bank has always served the common good. We want to continue this practise but make it more accessible to the public, irrespective of use. Many interesting details have been preserved on the roof and on the façade of the Frenkel building. We want to actively promote this by making the roof and the main entrance accessible to the public. The reconstruction of the main entrance also means adapting the building to meet modern standards. By adding a ramp on the outside and a lift inside, barrier-free access to the roof is ensured.

CURRENT SITUATION

The building is completely obscured by a protective wall and trees. It is not visible from the street. The ramp and stairs are unusable.

SUGGESTION

Add a usable ramp. Place the school's security checkpoint behind the original main entrance. Open up the edifice of the protective wall by making it half-height thereby freeing up the view of the rest of the building. Necessary changes in the plan to meet with modern usage standards.

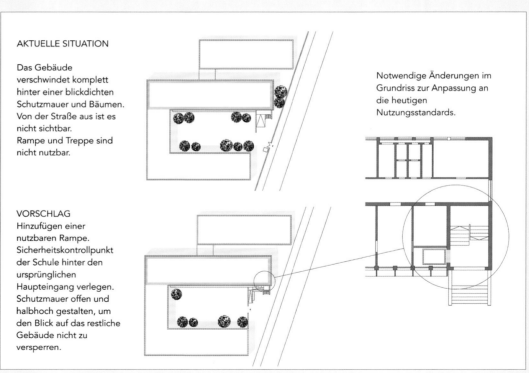

AKTUELLE SITUATION

Das Gebäude verschwindet komplett hinter einer blickdichten Schutzmauer und Bäumen. Von der Straße aus ist es nicht sichtbar. Rampe und Treppe sind nicht nutzbar.

Notwendige Änderungen im Grundriss zur Anpassung an die heutigen Nutzungsstandards.

VORSCHLAG
Hinzufügen einer nutzbaren Rampe. Sicherheitskontrollpunkt der Schule hinter den ursprünglichen Haupteingang verlegen. Schutzmauer offen und halbhoch gestalten, um den Blick auf das restliche Gebäude nicht zu versperren.

Original Details by Frenkel

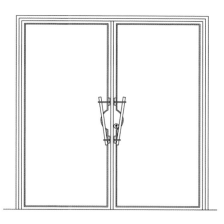

Blood Bank, Main Entrance

Blood Bank, Sun Shades

Attic

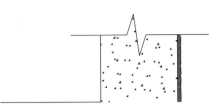

Natural Ventilation System

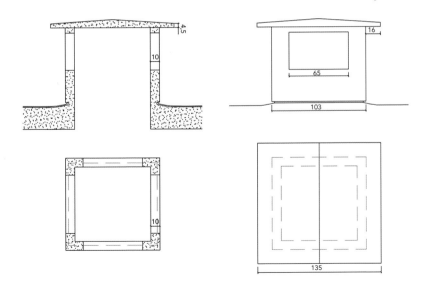

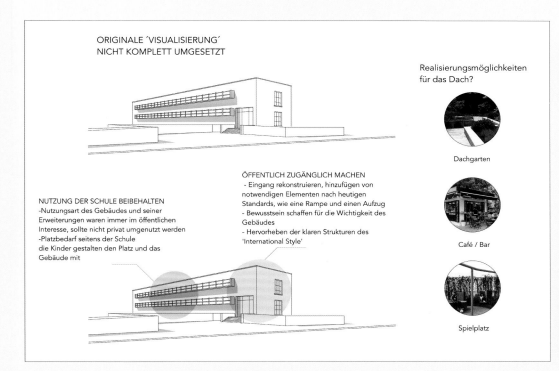

ORIGINALE ´VISUALISIERUNG´
NICHT KOMPLETT UMGESETZT

Realisierungsmöglichkeiten
für das Dach?

Dachgarten

Café / Bar

Spielplatz

ÖFFENTLICH ZUGÄNGLICH MACHEN
- Eingang rekonstruieren, hinzufügen von
notwendigen Elementen nach heutigen
Standards, wie eine Rampe und einen Aufzug
- Bewusstsein schaffen für die Wichtigkeit des
Gebäudes
- Hervorheben der klaren Strukturen des
'International Style'

NUTZUNG DER SCHULE BEIBEHALTEN
-Nutzungsart des Gebäudes und seiner
Erweiterungen waren immer im öffentlichen
Interesse, sollte nicht privat umgenutzt werden
-Platzbedarf seitens der Schule
die Kinder gestalten den Platz und das
Gebäude mit

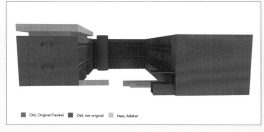

■ Old, Original Frenkel   ■ Old, not original   ▢ New, Addion

(from left to right:) **Shai Litvak and Keren Frizigon, Jerusalem,
Lena Schwinn, Mainz, Photo: Eléna Hinsch**

RETAIN THE CURRENT USE AS A SCHOOL

The designated use of the building and its
extensions was always a matter of public interest
and should therefore not be redeveloped for
private, commercial purposes
- the school needs more space; pupils participate
  in the design of both the space and the building
  itself

PROVISION OF PUBLIC ACCESS

- reconstruction of the entrance, addition of
  necessary features in keeping with the standards of the day, such as a ramp and a lift
- create and promote awareness of the building's
  architectural heritage and significance
- emphasise the clear structures of the International Style

USAGE POTENTIALS

- roof garden
- café/bar
- play ground

THE STUDENT´S WORKS
THE KIRYATI HOUSE

The Kiryati House – Project 1

Tamar Ben Israel, Jannes Beyer, Marlon Dina

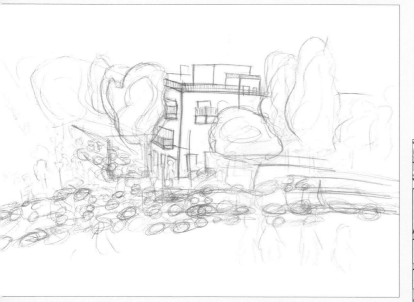

Our first impressions of the site (crowded, busy, noisy) as depicted in the sketches were confirmed.
Lots of movement/ traffic at the neighbouring intersection, including cars, buses, scooters, cyclists and pedestrians formed the distinctive atmosphere. In contrast to this, the yard seems calm and peaceful, emphasized by extensive greenery.
Consequently, our proposal deals with these two situations, which the site is exposed to.

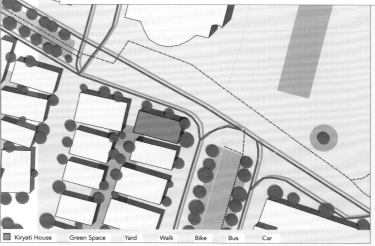

Kiryati House   Green Space   Yard   Walk   Bike   Bus   Car

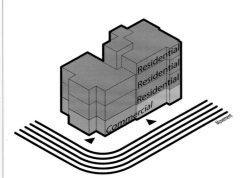

Old use: mostly residential, ground floor commercial

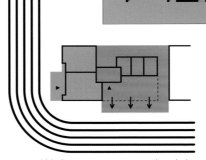

Old plan: open to street, enclosed plan

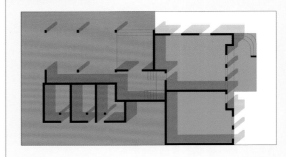

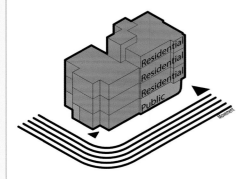

New use: Keep residential floors, add public area

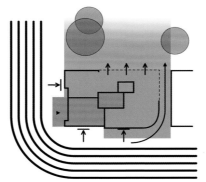

New plan: activate yard, open floor plan

(from left to right:) **Tamar Ben Israel, Jerusalem, Marlon Dina and Jannes Beyer, Braunschweig**, Photo: Eléna Hinsch

The Kiryati House – Project 2

Chen Gabay, Shir Sara Moallem,
Valerie Stillger

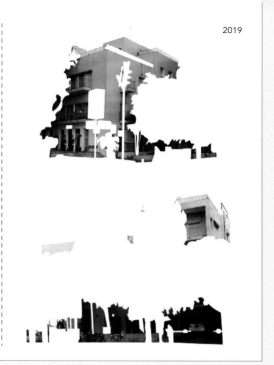

1938   2019

ADAPTION:

Inspired by the partly covered green areas of the two-storey Ya'akov garden complex and the interplay of light and shade, we developed a second, 'secret' retreat for locals as well as for adventure-loving tourists. Over the years, Mestetchkin's apartment has virtually disappeared behind large trees, partly neglected front gardens and immense volumes of traffic; it has long since ceased to do justice to its prominent position. Not least, the change in ownership and the big issue of the housing shortage in the city have definitely contributed significantly to this predicament.

We make use of this 'hidden place', turning a negative into a positive. The corner location should continue to attract the attention of more observant passersby, the glass floor further stimulating curiosity. The ground floor is completely open plan so that the remaining three storeys appear to 'float'. In order to annex the existing public space, a new lowered basement level is created via a representative staircase and ramp system.

Café, bar and exhibition space are harmoniously enveloped by a green canopy. The tress, shrubs and plants are to be preserved in their entirety and supplemented with indigenous regional and traditional plants in the fore garden area. This green canopy should not only be reflected on all sides of the façade, but also be found in the basement area and on the new roof garden storey. For this reason we have called our project: The Green Sandwich.

Since we are also dealing with two fundamentally separate structures accessed via a shared central stairwell, we envisage two discrete uses. The front section will be used for hotel purposes whereas the rear section will continue to be used residentially. Thus, the inside of building will also be accessible to the general public and provide a solution to the ongoing funding issue. There would be no major changes to the façade so that Mestechkin's original vision remains unaltered. The individual hotel apartments are to be accessed primarily via an external (glass) elevator situated on the front of the building, so that the residents remain unaffected. The roof terrace provides a shared green crown to complete the project and gives users the opportunity to escape the confined space, the traffic chaos and noise and immerse themselves in greenery.

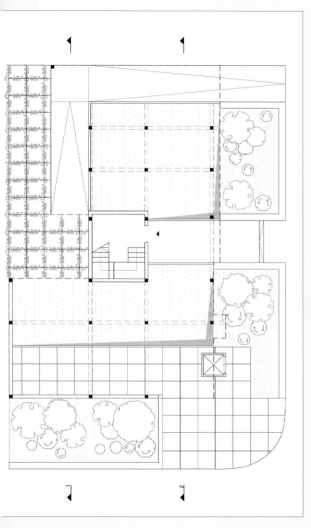

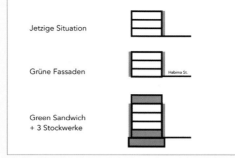

Jetzige Situation

Grüne Fassaden

Habima St.

Green Sandwich
+ 3 Stockwerke

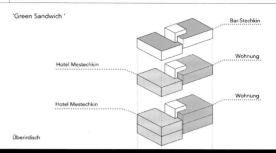

'Green Sandwich'

Bar-Stechkin

Hotel Mestechkin

Wohnung

Hotel Mestechkin

Wohnung

Überirdisch

Der Geheime Garten

Unterirdisch

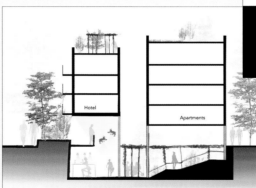

Hotel

Apartments

(from left to right:) **Valerie Stillger, Mainz, Chen Gabay and Shir Sara Moallem, Jerusalem,** Photo: Eléna Hinsch

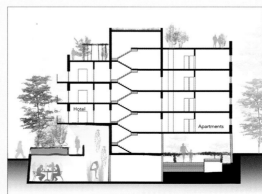

Hotel

Apartments

The Kiryati House – Project 3

Arne Müchler

ANSICHT M 1:100

Arne Müchler,
Mainz, Photo:
Eléna Hinsch

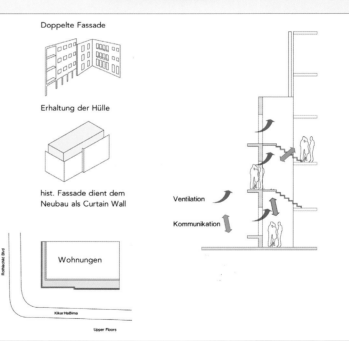

Doppelte Fassade

Erhaltung der Hülle

hist. Fassade dient dem
Neubau als Curtain Wall

Ventilation

Kommunikation

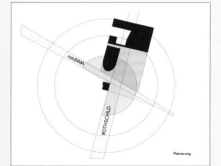

Platzierung

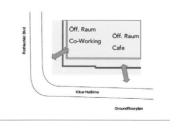

Öff. Raum
Co-Working
Öff. Raum
Cafe

Groundfloorplan

Wohnungen

Upper Floors

CONSERVATION WITHOUT HERITAGE PROTECTION CERTIFICATION

- retain the façade to preserve Mestechkin's design and typology;
- historic façade serves the new building as a Curtain Wall

- give the Mestechkin House a new use in keeping with new and developing urban requirements
- affordable apartments for young families, students and artists

- open the ground floor to the public (café, communal working space …)
- the upper storeys as a residential area, the gap in between as a communication portal

The Kiryati House – Project 4: From Dessau to Tel Aviv

Maya Nissan, Nelly Panchenko, Leopold Walther

Leopold Walther, Nelly Panchenko, Maya Nissan

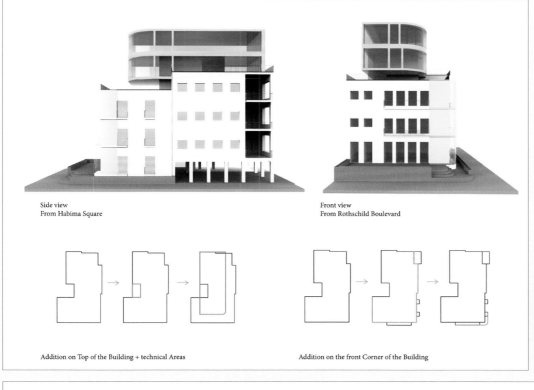

Side view
From Habima Square

Front view
From Rothschild Boulevard

Addition on Top of the Building + technical Areas

Addition on the front Corner of the Building

(from left to right:) **Maya Nissan, Jerusalem, Leopold Walther, Innsbruck, Nelly Panchenko, Jerusalem**

The Kiryati House

MORE THAN BAUHAUS

TEACHING ARCHITECTURE

REGINA STEPHAN

KNOWING WHAT YOU ARE DEALING WITH:
WHY THE HISTORY OF ARCHITECTURE IS IMPORTANT FOR ARCHITECTS

Students, whose actual primary desire is to design and build, generally regard the history of architecture and urban planning to be a subject area demanding intensive study and, initially at least, only opaquely relevant to their purpose. However, architectural studies are characterised by a wide range of different subjects, ranging from the classical disciplines of design and construction and reaching into other areas, including the history of architecture and urban planning, which, for its part, is also anchored in the study of art history, and thus the humanities.

Alongside the pure dissemination of knowledge regarding the genesis of architecture based on historical and geographical longitudinal and cross-sectional approaches, its specific task is the training of the eye for the conceptual and constructional characteristics, architectural subtleties and structural details that allow for a differentiation in the first place between different masters and how they are classified in terms of specific time periods and locational contexts – in Classical Antiquity, the Middle Ages and modern era, as well as in the present day. It is imperative that academic and terminological precision

in the approach to and treatment of buildings is harnessed to ensure a proper, considered discourse.

Inflationary usage of the term "Bauhaus architecture" in recent times lacks this very important aspect of diligence. One can scarcely escape it in the Bauhaus Centenary: estate agents are offering Bauhaus villas, Tel Aviv has – according to Wikipedia – "a collection of over 4,000 buildings built in a unique form of the Bauhaus or International style", and there's even a Europe-wide DIY chain of stores which calls itself Bauhaus. By contrast, in the history of architecture, the generic category "Bauhaus architecture" is not used and is applied only, if at all, to the buildings actually built by Bauhaus teachers and alumni.

As part of the two workshops held in Dessau and Tel Aviv, the task was to unravel the historical relationships and backstories of the selected buildings. Classical methods were used to this end: precise study and analysis of the buildings, archival and secondary literature studies on the respective architects, builders and construction projects, reconstruction of the original

concept and appearance with the aid of historical plans and photographic material, comparison with contemporary buildings or building that pre-dated them.

In order to relate the buildings in Tel Aviv to the theoretical teaching at the Staatliches Bauhaus, original Bauhaus buildings designed by Walter Gropius and Hannes Meyer between 1926 and 1930 were studied at the opening Dessau workshop: the school building, the Prellerhaus, the masters' houses, the Dessau-Törten housing scheme with Gropius' terraced houses and Meyer's balcony-access blocks of flats. In addition, there was a visit to the Building Research Archive (Bauforschungsarchiv) of the Bauhaus Dessau Foundation, which cast light on constructional detail.

A number of features are common to all Gropius buildings in the Dessau period: the smooth, white, plaster, external surfaces and the use in part of bold colours for the interior sections on smooth plaster, horizontal windows placed flush with the facade, spaciously projecting balconies with slender railings made of horizontal iron pipes, as well as flat roofs. In Meyer's case,

Working in the Bauforschungsarchiv,
Bauhaus Dessau Foundation,
Photo: Nathalie Wächter, 2018

access to the flats was via a connecting balcony or walkway. Unlike Gropius' buildings, Meyer's housing blocks with balcony access are clad in brick.

In Tel Aviv, the students worked in mixed groups on two buildings, which they scrutinised and explored using analytical tools of the history of architecture. As a result of the analysis, it could be verified that the buildings by Mestechkin and Frenkel – the objects of study – clearly indicate

the influence of Bauhaus theory and teaching on both architects: be it with regard to the type of floor plan and design for the façade, be it structural elements, such as staircases, balconies, railings. In addition, the renunciation of the otherwise ubiquitous round balconies in Tel Aviv with their characteristically generous outward trajectory can also be attributed to Bauhaus training, to which the comparison with the Dessau originals amply testifies.

ULRICH KNUFINKE

THE ETERNAL YOUTH OF MODERNISM
Aspects of cultural heritage conservation in Tel Aviv-Jaffa

One of the received opinions about modern architecture is that it cannot age "with dignity" – its materials and structures are not designed to last, indeed, this postmodern-romantic view on the lives of buildings even contradicts the basic idea of modernism, namely that buildings should exist beyond the set period of their intended use. It is seen as something ahistorical in keeping with the thinking of some modernist ideologues: antihistorical functionalism detached from the history of architecture engendering short life cycles for buildings and simultaneously giving rise to the myth of the eternal youth of modernism – demolition and replacement included. For whatever considered or unconsidered reasons, these structures have been legitimised as material, aesthetic and historical witnesses to our – emotionally speaking – positively-charged recent past, worthy of institutional veneration and preservation. Be that as it may, these now superannuated octogenarians either need a quick dip in the fountain of youth or receive some intelligent, careful conservation in order to be fit for posterity.

Around five decades after their construction, a number of modernist buildings in Tel Aviv were in a poor state of repair; subsequent extensions, additions and alterations (e.g. the closure of balconies, conversion of ground floor premises into shops, installation of air conditioning systems, etc.), but also the depredations of time have taken their toll on the erstwhile white and sandy-yellow, radiant image of the bourgeois garden city with its abundant greenery, leaving it looking forlorn, shabby and grey.

In spite of the White City's "shabby chic" appearance, architectural, historical and tourist interest in this extraordinary ensemble burgeoned during the 1980s, culminating in the bestowal of World Heritage status in 2003 by UNESCO. The "White City" World Heritage Site (and numerous other 1930s buildings outside the site within the Tel Aviv-Jaffa conurbation) demand highly differentiated concepts for the preservation and conservation of modern architecture. The large area and the high number of listed objects alone (around 4,000 buildings in the World Heritage zone, many hundreds outside, especially in Jaffa) are prime candidates for such differentiated concepts of protection and conservation. The increased attention paid to the buildings has coincided with a rapid transformation of Tel Aviv-Yafo. The development of the city into Israel's high-tech "boom-town" metropolis needs new living space and new office space even today. Life in the "Bauhaus" is fashionable, 1930s houses are in demand and of interest to speculators. Luxurious renovations, the addition of storeys and extensions are lucrative; in any case, the historic building materials and installations are in need of an upgrade after many decades of decline.

Under these circumstances, concepts for the conservation of the entire ensemble that aim at optimum material preservation of the original substance whilst simultaneously retaining the visibility of historical layers of change, are naturally enormously difficult to implement. In Tel Aviv-Yafo, the regulations governing the protection of historic monuments show considerable latitude: in the case of the vast majority of buildings, only the façades need to be preserved; owners are entitled to add a limited number of storeys, whereby such additions are graded according to the respective listed status of the building in question. The potential profit from an additional

storey is supposed to offset the cost of renovating the historic façade. In the case of a few particularly valuable buildings (currently around 120 properties), the addition of new storeys is to be avoided; here, the owners can sell their right to add a storey or transfer it to other buildings and thus finance the refurbishment.

This "multiclass heritage society" prevails and has both positive and negative corollaries: on the one hand, it has been possible to halt the degeneration of many properties, indeed, some of them have been renovated to exemplary standards; on the other, the additional storeys distort the overall proportions of the buildings and alter the scale of the cityscape – not to mention the loss of period features, especially windows, doors and fittings.

In the spring of 2019, the workshop consciously devoted its attention to two objects, which, given the current practice of listing heritage sites and the conservation of monuments in Tel Aviv-Yafo, should be regarded as particularly endangered, even though they are widely recognised as the work of Bauhaus

alumni. Neither Shmuel Mestechkin's Kiryati apartment block on Rothschild Boulevard erected in 1938 nor the former blood bank in Jaffa designed by Chanan Frenkel and built between 1953 and 1956 are listed. While the apartment block in Tel Aviv has undergone comparatively few changes and is still primarily used as a residential building, the blood bank in Jaffa has been rebuilt and extended on numerous occasions and currently houses a school. In spite of the fact that economic pressures and expediency in the near future might entail the demolition or radical alteration of the buildings without any objections on the part of conservationists holding

sway, measures to preserve them and technical upgrades are nevertheless underway.

The basis for a workable future concept for the conservation of these sites must include the preparation of a systematic documentation for both objects: a survey and archival studies, but also a collation of materials, surfaces, constructions, installations and fittings in terms of intensive building research/archaeology are necessary in order to isolate which elements of the buildings are worth preserving. Both the Kiryati House and the blood bank provide a wide spectrum of possible research questions ranging from design and materials to the study

Unrestored Building of the 1930s
with old additions on
King George Street, Tel Aviv,
Photo: Regina Stephan, 2019

of standardised elements and fittings. One of
the fundamental tasks for the students involved
in the Open Studio was to understand the
functional, material and constructional context
while observing and researching the objects in
situ, even if the compilation of a comprehensive
documentation was impossible in the limited
time available. However, building archaeology
in the sense described does not merely focus
on the "material" side of architecture, it aims to
understand the designs themselves and recognise the respective architects' underlying design
principles: this is effectively the only viable way
to "continue building", the only avenue left open
for the development of an adequate strategy
to manage inevitable modifications. By virtue of
the fact that their respective physical and spatial
structures are still intact and they can boast
many features (plastering, windows, doors,
light switches, etc.), both the Kiryati House
and the Jaffa blood bank present a wealth of
period architectural detail to be cherished. Their
integration into future conservation and utilisation
concepts is a challenge for users, designers and
conservationists alike.

As is the case with many other heritage and building research/archaeology initiatives in Tel Aviv-Yafo, the research undertaken in the workshop demonstrates that for heritage conservation in the long-term, a step-by-step compilation of an archive is indispensable in order to document the building archaeology of a given site, collect exemplary material and design samples, as well as assessing distinctive period features. The

Bauhaus Dessau Foundation's "Building Research Archive" is exemplary in this regard, which is why it was visited in November 2018 in the course of the Open Studio. The addition of a collection of model refurbishments and concomitant techniques exemplifying "best practice" would be desirable. Moreover, the undoubtedly prodigious task of conserving the legacy of international modernist architecture in Tel Aviv-Yafo should be perceived

fittingly as an undertaking on an international scale: cross-border and interdisciplinary cooperation in both research and education – to which the Open Studio would like to contribute beyond the Bauhaus Centenary year – can provide a template for this.

It is self-evident that the work of building archaeology and heritage conservation in Tel Aviv-Yafo (as is also the case elsewhere) is subject to enormous economic, political and time pressures: conversion, transformation and demolition continue apace; in many cases, the public awareness of heritage merely derives from marketing strategies; cementing the array of Tel Aviv-Yafo monuments in the consciousness of an interested public internationally will undoubtedly continue beyond 2019 and the Bauhaus Centenary. Nevertheless, the "eternal youth of modernism" dilemma persists: buildings are only ever considered "beautiful" in their new gloss – when these heritage objects age, as we must necessarily allow them to do, a second glance is necessary in order to comprehend their value fully.

SHMUEL GROAG

HOW WE TEACH CONSERVATION
Cultural Heritage methodology in the Department of Architecture at Bezalel

A conservation studio is regularly held at Bezalel in the fourth year for one semester and during the fifth year as part of a final project over the course of the year. The conservation unit, which I coordinate together with architect Shira Sprecher,

is set up to study urban space in Israel from the point of view of cultural heritage and its preservation, focusing on professional knowledge and contemporary discourse in the subject area. In our view, conservation should not be read as a

specialist field within architecture, the consideration of conservation as an important perspective is integral to any architectural project. Conservation-oriented planning as a method gives rise to more responsible and qualitatively enhanced additions to existing fabric and buildings.

The conservation unit focuses on the growing importance of conservation as an ethical and cultural system in which a given society can conduct ongoing discourse about its identity, as well as viewing conservation as a catalyst for cultural and socio-political change. For us, conservation is not conducted outside its cultural and political sphere, but is an integral part of architecture and the teaching of architecture. In recent years, the unit has formed a basis for discourse, working and research methods that place a special emphasis on the concept of "critical conservation". This conscious critical direction is a response to mainstream conservation practice, which is too hegemonic in its political bias and simultaneously creates over-designed conservation sites that in turn accelerate consumerism and gentrification processes. We seek to focus our study and research on the margins of

First Impressions Blood Bank

(next page:)
Studying Details in the Liebling House

Working in the Workshop

Basic Informations concerning additions in the White City,
All Photos: Eléna Hinsch

conservation, both in terms of the sites we are involved in – seeking an alternative to the current conservation mechanisms – and strengthening the link between conservation and the community. The search for the margins of conservation runs through all sections of the unit's activities, including historical research, planning processes and the development of the theoretical aspects of this topic. The research and intervention topics vary from year to year, and include, among other things, research into topic such as the Arab city, the ultra-Orthodox vernacular, the early Hebrew style, public housing and the preservation of Israeli modernism.

There are two new streams related to future endeavours in the conservation unit at Bezalel: the construction of a systematic archival body of knowledge for documentation and research, which has already been instigated, and the establishment of a conservation institute geared towards advanced academic degrees, as well as practical training in the field .

The purpose of the conservation studio, held in the fourth and fifth years of the study for a degree in architecture, is to acquire required

fields of knowledge, such as the historical and cultural analysis of the site, preparation of documentation and the connection between historical architectural research and architectural planning. The ultimate outcome of the studio in the fourth year is to plan an addition or extension to an existing structure. During the fifth year, the course of study is personal and requires individual students to choose a subject or on a site that contains a conservation-related issue or problem.

Running parallel to the practical studio, the students undergo a theoretical course that introduces them to the theory, problems and range of different practices in the field. As part of the preparatory work for the semester, the studio staff select the intervention area and prepare a list of optional sites for intervention. After an early tour, the students present an independent, free impression of the site which gives rise to discussion topics based the students' findings. It represents an essential aspect of the studio in the process of understanding the "significance" of the site as a basis to any intervention. This approach emphasises not only the aesthetic value of the historical structure itself, but also

places equal importance on the cultural heritage of the site and the personal stories of the past and present residents in all their social and political aspects.

In the first half of the semester, fourth-year students working in pairs engage in historical research and produce documentation files for the site they have chosen. A study of the building is undertaken as part of the documentation including drawing and documentation of the building's original details, cataloguing the techniques, crafts and skills that were current at the time of its construction. The focus on detail and techniques also comes to the fore in the final outcome of the work in the studio, where the students are also expected to present the significance based outcome, using contemporary technology and design.

For the fourth year studio, the relatively small scale of the selected buildings and the clear definition of how the various steps in the design process should progress enable students to present a high-calibre, architectural documentary survey coupled with a proposal for potential additions all within a thirteen-week semester.

KLAUS TRAGBAR
LEARNING AND WORKING ON SITE

The rapid increase in digitisation will certainly not have escaped anyone who has been closely monitoring the development of Western societies over the past twenty or thirty years. Nowadays virtually any and every piece of information can be accessed on the Internet. Sophisticated programmes allow us to sit in front of the screen at home and yet stroll through the major cities of the world, whereas other programmes and websites allow us to read up what there is to see there. Moreover, so-called e-learning is also *en vogue* at colleges and universities these days. Lectures are filmed and made available online, teaching materials are no longer provided in a handset, but are uploaded to an online learning platform, queries about courses are no longer posed in the lecture theatre, but are sent to the lecturers by e-mail.

A workshop in the field as it were, such as the "Spring School Tel Aviv - 100 Years of the Bauhaus 1919-2019", complete with supplementary excursions and discussions on site, would, at first glance, seem like a completely obsolete mode of teaching.

(left) **Puzzling out the complex building context and drawing locally**, Photo: Eléna Hinsch

(right) **Studying the built space**, Photo: Eléna Hinsch

respective author, photographer or editor. In a way, we are always looking through the eyes of others and not through our own. Of course, this also applies to the classic media such as books, magazines and even exhibitions, so that learning and working on site has always been a useful and necessary supplement to other formats.

Other techniques from the pre-digital era, such as drawing, also come into play when working and learning on site. Admittedly, drawing uses significantly more parts of the human body than, say, photography. The eye, which has to see something, the brain, which has to understand what the eye sees, the arm and the hand, which, controlled by the brain, now reproduce what has been seen and understood.

"You only see what you already know and understand", as Johann Wolfgang von Goethe already wisely observed, and even if he could scarcely have had our format of on-site learning and working in mind, his apt words describe well the process of seeing, recognising and understanding which is ultimately what it is all about.

Digitisation and on-site learning and working are by no means in competition with one another; on the contrary, they complement one another impeccably well. On-site learning and working simply cannot deliver the immediate, constant, on-demand availability of information of all kinds; on the other hand, direct visual apprehension, i.e. the ability to see and perceive architecture and urban planning situations gives learning and working on site an unmistakable quality absent in the digital world. The different play of light over the course of a day, the changes in the colours of a particular place, the sounds and smells that inhabit a place, in short: the ability to experience a place using all one's senses is irreplaceable. In addition, no matter how high-end and sophisticated the website might be, it always ever represents an interpretation on the part of the

PETRA MAYRHOFER

HISTORICAL BUILDING RESEARCH ON MODERNIST HERITAGE

The term "building research" – or building archaeology as it is also called – is generally closely associated with historical buildings, and as such, particularly with art-historically significant, conservation-worthy and, ideally, also listed objects. It is both necessary and useful to subject historical buildings to a thorough investigation in order to document their actual physical condition reliably, as there are either no extant plans for these objects – often several hundred years old – or the plans that do exist no longer correspond to the current state of the building due to various modifications over long periods of use. In particular, so-called vernacular architecture, i.e. buildings in rural areas – farms and outbuildings, but also residential buildings in an urban context, were mostly built in keeping with local practices and mostly entirely without plans.

Of course, the methodology of building research does not merely pertain to very old or architecturally-speaking especially valuable buildings, but can, in principle, be applied to any building in order to catalogue its current condition. Crucial to this undertaking, however,

is strictly the choice of the appropriate research method and tools for the object in question.

In essence, the starting point of any form of building research/archaeology is a thorough, accurate deformation monitoring and an exact, detailed structural survey of the respective building, effectively illustrating the current physical condition of the object with all additions and alterations to the floor plans, sections and aspects. Various methods are available for the purpose, ranging from analogue hand measurements using a tape measure, batter boards, spirit level and pencil drawings, via surveying with digital aids, such as laser distance meters and laser line levels, to highly technical equipment, such as total station theodolites, tachymeters and 3D-laser scanners. Even the deployment of drones fitted with onboard cameras can be useful for physically remote objects.

The choice of surveying method depends on a number of factors: the type and location of the researched structure, the intended purpose of the plans to be drawn up and ultimately on the available resources *in situ*. The combination of both analogue and digital methods can produce very

good results, whereby it is important to note that, generally speaking, more time should be allowed for on site drawings by hand. By contrast, the use of digital measuring devices, such as tachymeters and 3D-laser scanners, usually reduces the time spent working on site, albeit at the expense of time spent on post production on the computer, which is commensurately longer. However, it is paramount not to neglect personal contact with the object being researched, as small details and subtleties can only be recognised through close observation and scrutiny of the building on site. Details of this kind cannot be logged using digital surveying techniques alone. Usually, different methods and devices are combined in order to achieve a detailed and all-encompassing documentation and schematic survey of the respective object being researched.

When drawing up accurate deformation surveys and stone-by-stone floor plans, sections, aspects and detailed plans, care must be taken to record and represent the exact current physical condition of the building, with all possible damage and defects and without any supplements or conjectures. Choosing the appropriate

scale is a major factor in determining the density of information that can be displayed. It depends on the type and size of the object as well as the intended purpose of the structural drawings. Generally speaking, there are four levels in terms of accuracy, ranging from 1: 100 scale schematic surveys, to approximate realism at 1: 100 to 1:50 scale, to a detailed representation at 1:25 or 1:20 scale.

After a thorough survey of the object, a series of more detailed research activities follow. Here, the building is meticulously examined in terms of structure, construction method, materials and damage, possibly also sampled and photographed in detail. The plans produced during the surveys are indispensable for the subsequent translation of the archaeological investigation of the building into graphic form. For example, individual construction phases can be clearly illustrated in different colours and an overview of the building's age can be drawn up. Likewise, components and building phases can be displayed. A very important use of the plans is also the creation of various charts detailing

the different types of mortar and stone used, brick layers, traces of tool work, defects and, of course, material and structural damage. All the gathered data is subsequently collated in a structured way, thereby producing a comprehensive documentation of the object.

The plans and documentation arising from a survey and archaeological investigation of the building serve as a reliable basis for intended alterations to existing buildings, the most varied interventions or restoration measures for heritage sites, but also to answer a broad range of academic questions. They represent the starting point for further architectural studies.

APPENDIX
CURRICULA VITAE

SAMADAR AUKAL is an architect, born and raised in Shfar-am, Israel. She received her architecture degree from the Bezalel Academy of Arts and Design, Jerusalem. Her final project, which focused on the preservation of depopulated Palestinian villages, was presented as part of the "Conservation of Cultural Heritage" unit under the instruction of the architect Shmuel Groag. Since 2017 she has been working at an architecture and town planner's office in Jerusalem and as teaching assistant in Bezalel.

SHMUEL GROAG is an architect, town planner and conservation consultant. For many years he has been the head of the conservation unit and a senior lecturer at the department of architecture of the Bezalel Academy of Arts and Design in Jerusalem. Prior to this he was teaching conservation management at the Conservation Msc programme of the Technion in Haifa. He is a partner at Groag-Harel Architects, Conservation & Sustainable design, Tel Aviv. In 1978 Groag graduated the Technion in Haifa and in 2006 as Msc. the London School of Economics. He is a PHD candidate at the Ben Gurion University of the Negev on the subject of Heritage and conservation of Palestinian towns inside Israel.

SHARON GOLAN YARON is a conservation architect and the Programme director of the "White City Center" in the Liebling House in Tel Aviv, a cooperation between the Tel Aviv Municipality and the German government, initiated when she was working at the Conservation department of the Tel Aviv Municipality. She held numerous lectures around the world on the Subject of the International style in the Israeli context. She holds a bachelor's degree in Architecture from the IIT Chicago, a master's degree from the TU Berlin, and another master's degree in architectural conservation from the Technion in Haifa.

ELÉNA HINSCH is an art and architectural historian, graduated at the Ruprecht-Karls-University in Heidelberg 2012. In 2015 she got her master's degree in Heritage Conservation at the Otto-Frie-drich-University Bamberg. Since 2016 she has been working as a research associate at the institute of architecture of the Hochschule Mainz, University of Applied Sciences. She is writing her phD thesis on the residential buildings on the Mathildenhöhe in Darmstadt 1897-1914. Since December 2018 she is the city heritage conservationist in Bad Homburg vor der Höhe.

KATRIN KESSLER is an architect. She received her PhD from the Technische Universität Braunschweig. Her research field is the architecture of the European synagogues. For many years she has been working for the Bet Tfila – Research Unit for Jewish Architecture in Europe. She has been researching at the Center for Jewish Art of the Hebrew University Jerusalem. At present she is the head of the research project „Objects and spaces as reflections of religious practice in Jewish communities: Traditions and transformations of Jewry in Germany after the Shoa".

ULRICH KNUFINKE studied architecture and German literature at the Technische Universität Braunschweig. His Ph.D.-thesis on German Jewish cemetery architecture was published in 2007. For many years Knufinke was researcher and lecturer at the Bet Tfila – Research Unit for Jewish Architecture at the Technische Universität Braunschweig. Since 2018 he is senior lecturer (Privatdozent) there and works for the monuments preservation authority of the federal state of Lower Saxony (Niedersächsisches Landesamt für Denkmalpflege, Hannover).

VLADIMIR LEVIN has been the director of the Center for Jewish Art at the Hebrew University of Jerusalem since 2011. Educated in Saint Petersburg and Jerusalem, he received his phD in 2007. He worked as a research fellow in Beer Sheva, Leipzig and Southhampton. From 1993 to 2011 he joined the Center for Jewish Art as historian, archivist, coordinator of the architectural section and publications coordinator.

SHIRA LEVY BENYEMINI is an architect and city planner. She works as the Director of the White City Center at the Liebling House. She has an M.A. in City Planning from the Hebrew University in Jerusalem and is an expert on urban regeneration processes, community planning, and conservation. Levy Benyemini explores the interconnections of urban transformation, particularly involving cultural and artistic activities.

MONIKA MARKGRAF is an architect working as a research associate for the Bauhaus Dessau Foundation. She is responsible for building research and preservation. Prior to that, she worked as an architect with a focus on building research and the renovation of listed buildings. She is particularly interested in the architecture and history of the Bauhaus buildings as well as in their preservation and maintenance. The Bauforschungsarchiv of the Bauhaus Dessau Foundation, a building research archive, is a further key point of her work.

PETRA MAYRHOFER is an architect and archaeologist, graduated at the Technische Universität Wien and the University of Vienna. Since 2007 she has been participating yearly at the ÖAI (Austrian Archaeological Institute) excavations of Ephesos. From 2010 to 2014 she has been working as a research assistant at the institute for the cultural history of antiquity at the ÖAW (Austrian Academy of Science). Since 2013 Mayrhofer is the project manager of the ÖAI excavation of the Hamam IV in Ephesos/Selçuk. She is teaching at the University of Innsbruck, Institute architectural theory and building history.

REGINA STEPHAN is an art and architectural historian. A graduate of the Ludwig-Maximilians-University, Munich, she earned her doctorate in 1992 with her thesis on Erich Mendelsohn's Department Stores in Germany. She has taught at the University of Stuttgart and the Technische Universität Darmstadt, where she worked from 2000 to 2008 as a Postdoc at the Institute for History and Theory of Architecture. Stephan has been Professor of Architectural History at Hochschule Mainz, University of Applied Sciences, since 2008. The German Ministry of Interior and Building appointed her in the advisory board White City, Tel Aviv, and the commission „Building and planning in National-Socialism premises, institution outcomes".

KLAUS TRAGBAR studied architecture in Darmstadt and received his phD in 1997 with a thesis on medieval housing in Tuscany. He taught in Darmstadt, Mainz and Frankfurt am Main. From 1998 to 2001 Tragbar was Managing Director of the German Castle Association, from 2002 to 2013 Professor for Design, and Architectural History and Theory at the Augsburg University of Applied Sciences. Since February 2013 he has been Professor of Architecture, Architectural History and Monument Conservation at the University of Innsbruck. He is Head of the Archive of Building Arts.

APPENDIX

TUTORS, LECTURERS AND CONTRIBUTORS TO THE WORKSHOP

Leading team: Prof. Dr. Regina Rose Stephan, Shmuel Groag Msc., Prof. Dr. Klaus Tragbar, Dr. Ulrich Knufinke, Dr. Kartrin Kessler and Dr. Vladimir Levin
Assistance: Samadar Aukal, Eléna Hinsch, Petra Mayrhofer

Who	Institution	Contribution
Frank, Vinzenz	Bauhaus Dessau Foundation	Tour: Bauhaus and Master Houses Dessau
Möller, Werner	Bauhaus Dessau Foundation	Lecture: From Building Culture to Bauhaus Culture
Markgraf, Monika	Bauhaus Dessau Foundation	Lecture: Conservation policy of the Bauhaus in Dessau
Markgraf, Monika	Bauhaus Dessau Foundation	Visit of the Bauhaus and the Master houses
Bittner, Regina	Bauhaus Dessau Foundation	Lecture: Teaching Concepts of the Bauhaus
Markgraf, Monika	Bauhaus Dessau Foundation	Visit of the Housing Estate Dessau Törten
Markgraf, Monika	Bauhaus Dessau Foundation	Visit of the Bauforschungsarchiv Stiftung Bauhaus Dessau
Stephan, Regina	Hochschule Mainz University of Applied Sciences	Lecture: History of the City Dessau
Groag, Shmuel	Bezalel Academy Jerusalem	Tour of the White City
Golan, Sharon	White City Center Tel Aviv	Lecture: Conservation and General Planning History of Tel Aviv
Levin, Micha	Jerusalem	Lecture: The White City and the Bauhaus
Golan, Sharon	White City Center Tel Aviv	Tour of the White City Center
Efrat, Zvi	Bezalel Academy Jerusalem	Comments
Jeremie Hoffmann	Municipality of Tel Aviv Conservation Department	Lecture: Buildings rights and other conditions for conserving the White City
Yasky, Yuval	Bezalel Academy Jerusalem	Lecture: From the White City to the Kibbuz
Kiryati, Yehudith	Israel Development & Building Co. Ltd	Talk: Kiryati House Tel Aviv
Cohen, Esther	Bauhaus Gallery Tel Aviv	Tour: Exhibition in the Bauhaus Gallery
Tragbar, Klaus	Universität Innsbruck	Lecture: Building Additions in Europe (at least some of them …)
Regina Stephan	Hochschule Mainz University of Applied Sciences	Lecture: The Bauhaus, its predecessors and contemporary architects of the New Building in Germany
Knufinke, Ulrich	Lower Saxony State Office for the Preservation of Cultural Heritage, Hannover	Lecture: Ze'ev Haller
Knufinke, Ulrich	Lower Saxony State Office for the Preservation of Cultural Heritage, Hannover	Tour: West Jerusalem
Tragbar, Klaus	Universität Innsbruck	Presentation: 100 Years of Planning and Building in Palestine and Israel. A Research Proposal
Levin, Vladimir	Hebrew University, Center for Jewish Art, Jerusalem	Tour: Old City of Jerusalem
Jahn, Hartmut	Hochschule Mainz University of Applied Sciences	Supervision of the production of the documentary film

APPENDIX
PICTURE CREDITS

Bauhaus Dessau Foundation, Dessau   **29, 30 left + middle, 32, 35, 36, 37, 39, 127**

Bauhaus-Archiv, Berlin   **26**

Building Archive, Municipality of Tel Aviv-Yafo   **58 right**

Chemollo, Alessandra   **96**

City Engineer Archive, Municipality of Tel Aviv-Yafo   **82, 83, 85, 91, 92, 93, 94**

Groag Harel Architects, Tel Aviv   **63, 71 left + middle**

Groag, Shmuel   **66 right**

Hauptstaatsarchiv Nordrhein-Westfalen   **34**

Hinsch, Eléna   **71, 76, 77, 78, 80, 99 right, 102 bottom, 107 bottom, 108 bottom, 113 right, 116 bottom, 119 bottom, 120 top, 123 right**

Institut Mathildenhöhe, Darmstadt   **18/19**

Janericloebe über commons.wikimedia.org/wiki/File: Berlin_Neues_Museum_001.JPG   **97 top**

Knufinke, Ulrich   **53, 54, 55, 56, 57, 59, 61, 81, 87, 88, 89**

Kunstbibliothek Staatliche Museen zu Berlin   **17, 20 left**

Mainz, Anni, Das ist Tel Aviv, 1934   **58 left**

Matson (G. Eric and Edith) Photograph Collection, Library of Congress, Washington D.C.   **64**

Mercedes Benz Classic   **20 right**

National Library, Jerusalem   **65 right**

Participants of the Workshop   **41-49, 98-123**

Preiss, Ludwig, Palästina und das Ostjordanland, 1925   **62, 66 left**

Private Collection   **52**

Stephan, Regina   **21, 33, 95, 129, 130, 131**

Stock, Wolfgang Jean (Hg.): Architektur und Fotografie. Korrespondenzen. Basel 2002   **97 bottom right**

Tragbar, Klaus   **10, 97 bottom left**

Van Amstel, Frederick   **25**

VG Bildkunst   **23 left, 30 right**

Werner Durth, Darmstadt   **23 right, 24**

White City Center, Tel Aviv   **8, 72, 73, 74, 75**

APPENDIX

SELECTED BIBLIOGRAPHY

Bar-Or, Galia, *Kibbuz und Bauhaus. Pioniere des Kollektivs*, Bauhaus Taschenbuch 3, Dessau/Leipzig 2012.

Bauhaus-Archiv Berlin (ed.), *bauhaus global, Gesammelte Beiträge der Konferenz bauhaus global vom 21. bis 26. September 2009*, Neue Bauhausbücher vol. 3, Berlin 2010.

Bauhaus Achive, ed., Der vorbildliche Architekt. Mies van der Rohe. Architekturunterricht 1930-1958 am Bauhaus und in Chicago, exh. cat. Bauhaus-Archiv Museum für Gestaltung, Berlin, 1986.

Butter, Andreas, *Die unsichtbare Bauhausstadt. Eine Spurensuche in Dessau*, Bauhaus Taschenbuch 9, Dessau/Leipzig 2013.

Efrat, Zvi, *The Object of Zionism. The Architecture of Israel*, Leipzig 2018.

Engelmann, Christine, and Christian Schädlich, *Die Bauhausbauten in Dessau,* Berlin [1]1991, [2]1998.

Federal Institute for Research on Building, Urban Affairs and Spatial Development (BBSR) (ed.), *Tel Aviv White City: Modernist buildings in Israel and Germany. A project within the research programme "Future Building"* conducted by the German Federal Ministry for the Environment, Nature Conservation, Building and Nuclear Safety, Troisdorf 2015.

Fiedler, Jeannine, *Social utopias of the twenties: Bauhaus, Kibbutz, and the dream of a new man,* Wuppertal, 1995.

Fiedler, Jeannine, and Peter Feierabend, *Bauhaus,* Cologne 1999.

Gebeßler, August (ed.), *Meisterhaus Muche-Schlemmer. Die Geschichte einer Instandsetzung,* Stuttgart 2003.

Golan Yaron, Sharon, *100 Years of Bauhaus, 100 buildings,* Berlin 2019.

Gropius, Walter, *Idee und Aufbau des Staatlichen Bauhauses Weimar,* Munich, Weimar, 1923.

Gropius, Walter, *bauhausbauten dessau,* Fulda 1930, Reprint: [1]Mainz 1974, [2]Berlin 1997.

Gross, Micha (ed.), *Tel Aviv. Tel Aviv Views. Photos by Avraham Soskin and Ran Erde, 1909-2009,* Tel Aviv 2010.

Groag, Shmuel, "Lubya in Lavie Forest- on Conservation of the Palestinian Built Heritage in Israel", in: *Memory oblivion and construction of space,* edited by Tovi Fenster and Haim Jacobi, Van Leer Institute Jerusalem 2011, p. 177-209 (in Hebrew).

Groag, Shmuel, Invisible Conservation – Between destructible conservation and obliteration. *The Israeli Pavilion Catalogue,* Architecture Biennale, Venice, 2008

Groag, Shmuel, "Conservation and Oblivion", *Block 04 - Temporal Cities,* p 33-36, 2007 (in Hebrew)

Hyman, Benjamin, *British Planners in Palestine, 1918-1936,* A Thesis submitted for the degree of Ph.D. The London School of Economics and Political Science, 1994.

ICOMOS, Nationalkomitee der Bundesrepublik Deutschland (ed.), *Konservierung der Moderne? Über den Umgang mit Zeugnissen der Architekturgeschichte des 20. Jahrhunderts,* Tagungsbericht, Hefte des Deutschen Nationalkomitees, Vol. XXIV, München 1996.

Institut für Auslandsbeziehungen Stuttgart (ed.), *Tel Aviv. Neues Bauen 1930-1939.* Photographien Irmel Kamp-Bandau, Kat. Ausst., Tübingen 1993.

James-Chakraborty, Kathleen (ed.), *Bauhaus Culture. From Weimar to the Cold War,* Minneapolis 2006.

Knufinke, Ulrich, *Beiträge zur Geschichte der jüdischen Architektur.* Stuttgart 2015 (=Habilitationsschrift, masch.Man.).

Knufinke, Ulrich, "Jewish Ways to Architecture between Weimar Republic, National Socialism and Emigration: Questions for Future Inter-disciplinary Research in the Field of Jewish Architecture", in: Keßler, Katrin und Alexander von Kienlin (eds.): *Jewish Architecture. New Sources and Approaches*, Petersberg 2015, S.151-159 (with Sylvia Necker).

Knufinke, Ulrich, *Bauhaus: Jerusalem*, Tel Aviv 2012.

Levin, Michael, *Modern Architecture in Israel*, Milan 2005.

LeVine, Mark, *Overthrowing Geography. Jaffa, Tel Aviv, and the struggle for Palestine, 1880-1948*, Berkeley 2005.

LeVine, Mark, "Planning to conquer: Modernity and its antinomies in the New-Old Jaffa", in: *Constructing a Sense of Place: Architecture and the Zionist Discourse*, edited by Haim Yacobi, Burlington 2004.

Lietz, Bettina, and Markgraf, Monika, *Architekturoberflächen*, Berlin 2004.

Lin, Nimrod, *Deconstructing Jaffa*, Tel Aviv 2011

Markgraf, Monika (ed.), *Archäologie der Moderne. Sanierung Bauhaus Dessau*, Berlin 2006

Markgraf, Monika, and Andreas Schwarting, *Bauforschungsarchiv Stiftung Bauhaus Dessau*, edited by Bauhaus Dessau Foundation, Dessau 2007

Markgraf, Monika, *Die Dessauer Bauhausbauten*, Bauhaus Taschenbuch 16, Dessau/Leipzig 2016.

Matz, Reinhard, and Andreas Schwarting, eds, *The Disappearance of the Revolution in Renovation. The History of the Gropius Settlement Dessau-Törten (1926-2011)*, Berlin 2011.

Metzger-Szmuk, Nitza, *Dwelling on the Dunes: Tel Aviv, Modern Movement and Bauhaus ideals*, Paris 2004

Meyer, Edina, „Oskar Kaufmanns Habimah-Theater in Tel Aviv", in: *Architektur, Stadt und Politik*, edited by Burkhard Bergius, Janos Frecot, Dieter Radicke, Gießen 1979.

Rotbard, Sharon, *White City, Black City. Architecture and War in Tel Aviv and Jaffa*, Cambridge 2015.

Schwarting, Andreas, *Die Siedlung Dessau-Törten*, Bauhaus Taschenbuch 7, Dessau/Leipzig 2017.

Sharon, Arieh, *Kibbutz + Bauhaus, An Architect's way in a New Land*, Stuttgart and Tel Aviv, 1976

Sonder, Ines, and Werner Möller, Ruwen Egri, *Vom Bauhaus nach Palästina. Chanan Frenkel, Ricarda und Heinz Schwerin*, Bauhaus Taschenbuch 6, Dessau/Leipzig 2013.

Stephan, Regina (ed.), *Eric Mendelsohn. Architect 1887-1953*. New York 1999

Thöner, Wolfgang, and Monika Markgraf, *Die Meisterhäuser in Dessau*, Bauhaus Taschenbuch 10, Dessau/Leipzig 2014.

Tzur, Moki, and Yuval Daniaeli, *Mestechkin Builds Israel: Architecture in the Kibbutz*, (in Hebrew), Bnei Brak 2008.

Wahrhaftig, Myra, *Sie legten den Grundstein. Leben und Wirken deutschsprachiger jüdischer Architekten in Palästina 1918-1948*, Tübingen, Berlin 1996.

Yagid-Haimovici, Meira, *Dov Karmi: Architect-Engineer Public Domestica*, (in Hebrew), Tel Aviv, 2001.

Yasky, Yuval, "Neither City, Nor Village – A Kibbutz", in: *Kibbutz: Architecture without Precedents*, edited by Galia Bar Or and Yuval Yaski, Catalogue of the Israeli pavilion at the 12th International Architecture Biennale in Venice, 2010